Downtown 2

English for Work and Life

EDWARD J. MCBRIDE

Australia • Brazil • Japan • Korea • Mexico • Singapore • Spain • United Kingdom • United States

Downtown 2: English for Work and Life
Edward J. McBride

Publisher, Adult and Academic ESL:
James W. Brown

Senior Acquisitions Editor, Adult and
Academic: Sherrise Roehr

Director of Product Development:
Anita Raducanu

Development Editor: Kasia McNabb

Development Editor: Amy Lawler

Director of Product Marketing: Amy Mabley

Senior Field Marketing Manager:
Donna Lee Kennedy

Product Marketing Manager: Laura Needham

Editorial Assistant: Katherine Reilly

Senior Production Editor: Maryellen E. Killeen

Senior Print Buyer: Mary Beth Hennebury

Photo Researcher: Christina Micek

Indexer: Alexandra Nickerson

Proofreader: Maria Hetu

Design and Composition:
Jan Fisher/Publication Services

Cover Design: Lori Stuart

Cover Art: Jean-François Allaux

Interior Art: Jean-François Allaux, Mona Mark,
Scott MacNeill, Dave Sullivan

Library of Congress Number: 2004047869

Domestic ISBN-13: 978-0-8384-4379-8

ISE ISBN-13: 978-1-4130-1543-0

National Geographic Learning
20 Channel Center Street
Boston, MA 02210
USA

Cengage Learning is a leading provider of customized learning solutions with office locations around the globe, including Singapore, the United Kingdom, Australia, Mexico, Brazil, and Japan.

Cengage Learning products are represented in Canada by Nelson Education, Ltd.

Visit National Geographic Learning online at **elt.heinle.com**

Visit our corporate website at **cengage.com**

Printed in the United States of America
13 14 15 16 20 19 18 17

Dedication

To all the wonderful students who have given me, over the years, at least as much as I have given them.

Acknowledgments

The author and publisher would like the thank the following reviewers for the valuable input:

Elizabeth Aderman
New York City Board of Education
New York, NY

Jolie Bechet
Fairfax Community Adult School
Los Angeles, CA

Cheryl Benz
Georgia Perimeter College
Clarkston, GA

Chan Bostwick
Los Angeles Unified School District
Los Angeles, CA

Patricia Brenner
University of Washington
Seattle, WA

Clif de Córdoba
Roosevelt Community Adult School
Los Angeles, CA

Marti Estrin
Santa Rosa Junior College
Santa Rosa, CA

Judith Finkelstein
Reseda Community Adult School
Reseda, CA

Lawrence Fish
Shorefront YM-YWHA
    English Language Program
Brooklyn, NY

Giang Hoang
Evans Community Adult School
Los Angeles, CA

Arther Hui
Mount San Antonio College
Walnut, CA

Renee Klosz
Lindsey Hopkins Technical
    Education Center
Miami, FL

Carol Lowther
Palomar College
San Marcos, CA

Barbara Oles
Literacy Volunteers of
    Greater Hartford
Hartford, CT

Pamela Rogers
Phoenix College
Phoenix, AZ

Eric Rosenbaum
BEGIN Managed Programs
New York, NY

Stan Yarbro
La Alianza Hispana
Roxbury, MA

Contents

Contents

Contents

Contents

Contents

Contents

EFF	CASAS	LAUSD Beginning	Florida LCP-B	Texas LCP-B
Many EFF skills are practiced in this chapter, with a particular focus on: • Working together • Providing leadership • Guiding others • Seeking guidance and support • Expressing sense of self • Respecting others • Creating and pursuing goals • Speaking so others can understand	• **Lesson 1:** 0.1.2, 0.1.3, 0.2.4, 2.3.2, 2.7.1, 4.8.1 • **Lesson 2:** 0.1.4, 0.2.4, 1.1.5, 2.3.3, 4.8.1, 4.8.5, 4.8.6 • **Lesson 3:** 0.2.3, 1.1.3, 1.2.5, 2.2.4, 2.6.3, 4.8.1, 4.8.3, 7.4.1, 6.7.2	**Competencies:** 2, 7b, 9a, 9b, 9c, 62, 64, 26 **Grammar:** 5a, 21a, 26, 28a, 27, 29, 30a	• **Lesson 1:** 4.05.04, 4.15.02, 4.15.03, 4.15.09, 4.15.13, 4.16.02, 4.16.03, 4.16.08 • **Lesson 2:** 4.13.01, 4.13.02, 4.15.01, 4.15.02, 4.15.03, 4.15.09, 4.15.13, 4.16.02, 4.16.07, 4.16.08 • **Lesson 3:** 4.04.01, 4.05.04, 4.09.03, 4.09.04, 4.11.01, 4.15.01, 4.15.02, 4.15.03, 4.15.16, 4.15.17, 4.16.02, 4.16.08, 4.17.02, 4.17.04	• **Lesson 1:** 22.01, 22.03, 26.01, 29.03 • **Lesson 2:** 30.01 • **Lesson 3:** 26.01, 26.02
Many EFF skills are practiced in this chapter, with a particular focus on: • Working together • Providing leadership • Guiding others • Seeking guidance and support • Listening actively • Observing critically • Speaking so others can understand	• **Lesson 1:** 0.1.3, 1.1.3, 1.3.7, 2.2.1, 2.5.4, 4.8.1, 4.8.6, 6.7.2 • **Lesson 2:** 0.1.3, 4.7.4, 4.8.1, 4.8.6, 7.2.4, 7.4.1 • **Lesson 3:** 0.2.3, 1.2.1, 1.2.2, 1.2.3, 1.3.2, 1.3.3, 1.2.5, 1.6.3, 4.8.1, 4.8.3, 7.4.1	**Competencies:** 32, 33, 30, 62a, 62b **Grammar:** 4, 15, 20c, 20d, 27	• **Lesson 1:** 4.05.04, 4.15.02, 4.15.03, 4.15.09, 4.15.13, 4.16.02, 4.16.03, 4.16.08 • **Lesson 2:** 4.13.01, 4.13.02, 4.15.01, 4.15.02, 4.15.03, 4.15.09, 4.15.13, 4.16.02, 4.16.07, 4.16.08 • **Lesson 3:** 4.04.01, 4.05.04, 4.09.03, 4.09.04, 4.11.01, 4.15.01, 4.15.02, 4.15.03, 4.15.16, 4.15.17, 4.16.02, 4.16.08, 4.17.02, 4.17.04	• **Lesson 1:** 26.03, 32.07, 33.07 • **Lesson 2:** 33.07 • **Lesson 3:** 22.01, 28.03, 33.07
Many EFF skills are practiced in this chapter, with a particular focus on: • Working together • Providing leadership • Guiding others • Seeking guidance and support • Listening actively • Observing critically • Negotiating • Reading with understanding • Conveying ideas in writing	• **Lesson 1:** 3.1.1, 3.1.2, 3.3.1, 7.4.1 • **Lesson 2:** 1.2.5, 3.3.2, 3.3.3, 4.8.1, 4.8.6 • **Lesson 3:** 0.2.3, 1.9.1, 2.2.2, 3.2.1, 3.4.1, 3.4.2, 4.3.1, 4.3.4, 4.6.2, 4.8.1, 4.8.2, 4.8.6, 7.4.1	**Competencies:** 10a, 10b, 11e, 41, 43, 44, 45a, 45b, 46, 47, 55a, 57, 62b **Grammar:** 6a, 6b, 11b, 13, 28a, 29	• **Lesson 1:** 4.05.04, 4.09.02, 4.11.01, 4.11.09, 4.15.01, 4.15.02, 4.15.03, 4.15.06, 4.15.08, 4.15.13, 4.15.16, 4.16.02, 4.16.03, 4.16.08 • **Lesson 2:** 4.07.06, 4.09.01, 4.09.06, 4.10.01, 4.15.01, 4.15.02, 4.15.03, 4.15.09, 4.16.02 • **Lesson 3:** 4.02.02, 4.02.03, 4.05.01, 4.16.03, 4.07.04, 4.07.07, 4.07.09, 4.10.01, 4.15.01, 4.15.02, 4.15.03, 4.15.13, 4.15.16, 4.15.17, 4.16.02, 4.16.08, 4.17.02	• **Lesson 1:** 24.01, 24.03, 24.04, 24.06 • **Lesson 2:** 19.01, 26.06, 27.02 • **Lesson 3:** 19.01, 24.02, 24.04

Contents

Contents

To the Teacher

Attempting to learn a new language can often be challenging and even frustrating. But learning English should also be fun. That's the idea I was given by the wonderful administrator who hired me twelve years ago to teach my first ESL class. She took me aside as I was about to walk nervously into class for the first time. "Make your students comfortable," she said. "Make the class fun. And teach them what they really need to know."

Twelve years of teaching and about ten thousand students later, these simple, yet essential, ideas have become guiding pedagogical principles for me. In each of my classes, I have striven to teach students what they need to know, in a way that is both comfortable and enjoyable. Ultimately, that's the philosophy behind *Downtown*, too. The simplicity of the layout of each page, along with the logical, slow-paced progression of the material makes it a comfortable text for both teachers and students to use. I've included a wide variety of activities, as well as playful features like "Game Time" and a chapter-concluding cartoon, to make *Downtown 2* an enjoyable text to use. And, by developing the text with a focus on standards-based competencies, I've sought to teach students the information they most need to know.

This four-level, competency-based series is built around the language skills students need to function in both their everyday lives and in the workplace, while giving a good deal of attention to grammar. It is a general ESL text that pays more attention to work-related language needs than is typical. The goal of the text is to facilitate student-centered learning in order to lead students to real communicative competence.

The first page of each chapter of *Downtown 2* presents an overview of the material of the chapter in context, using a picture-dictionary format. This is followed by three lessons, with the third lesson focusing on work-related English. Many of the structures and key concepts are recycled throughout the lessons, with the goal of maximizing student practice. Each lesson is carefully scaffolded to progress from guided practice to more communicative activities in which students begin to take more control of their own learning.

Each chapter concludes with a Chapter Review, which provides material that practices and synthesizes the skills that students have been introduced to in the previous three lessons. The review culminates in a "Teamwork Task" activity. This activity gives students the opportunity to work together to apply the skills they have learned to complete a real world type of task. At the end of each chapter you will find a *Downtown* cartoon—a humorous, serial-style cartoon, which invites students to practice the vocabulary and grammar presented in the chapter.

Each chapter presents a variety of activities that practice grammar, as well as reading, writing, listening, and speaking skills. Problem-solving activities are also included in many lessons, and are particularly emphasized at the higher levels.

The material in **Downtown 2** is presented in real-life contexts. Students are introduced to vocabulary, grammar, and real-world skills through the interactions of a cast of realistic, multiethnic characters who function as parents, workers, and community members in their own "downtown" world.

My intention in developing **Downtown 2** was to provide an easy-to-use text, brimming with essential and enjoyable language learning material. I hope **Downtown 2** succeeds in this and that it helps to cultivate an effective and motivating learning atmosphere in your classroom. Please feel free to send me your comments and suggestions at ngl.cengage.com. Ancillary material includes Teacher's Editions, workbooks, audio cassettes/CDs, transparencies, and an *ExamView® Pro* assessment CD-Rom containing a customizable test bank for each level.

Downtown: English for Work and Life

Downtown offers a well-balanced approach that combines a standards-based and a grammar-based syllabus. This gives English learners the comprehensive language skills they need to succeed in their daily lives, both at home and at work.

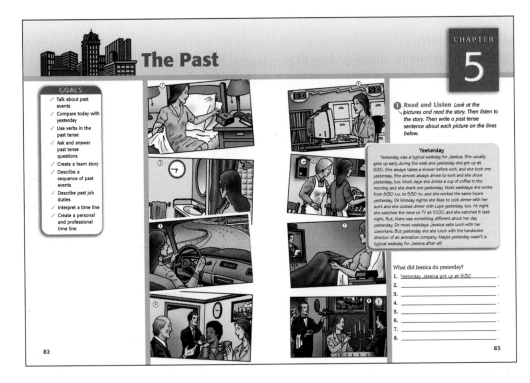

- **Picture dictionary-style chapter openers** introduce vocabulary in context and outline chapter goals.

- **Audio Tapes and CDs** enhance learning through dialogues, listening practice, readings, and pronunciation exercises.

- **Theme-based chapters include three lessons.** The third lesson in each chapter focuses on the skills and vocabulary necessary for the workplace.

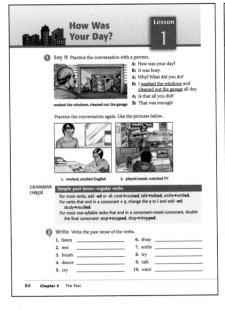

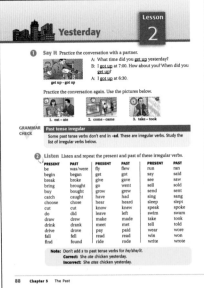

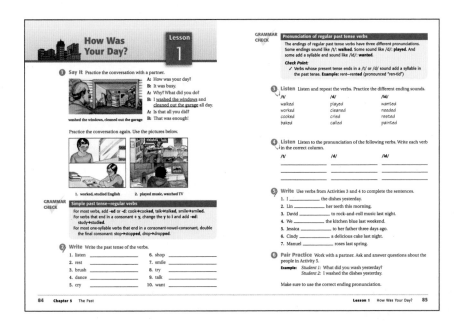

- **The strong grammar syllabus** supports the integrated language learning focus.

- **The lives of recurring characters provide the context** for a variety of activities such as *Grammar Check, Say It, Game Time,* and other communicative items.

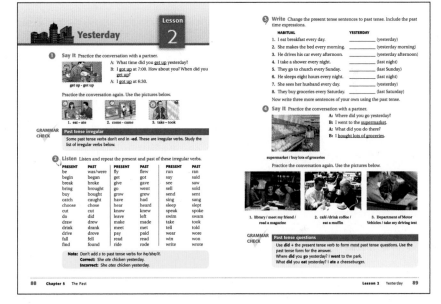

- **Problem solving activities** engage students' critical thinking.

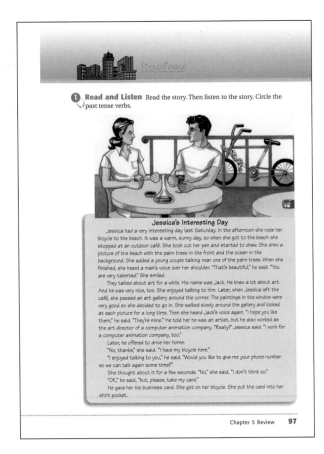

- **Review pages** practice all skills learned in the chapter and let students synthesize what they have learned.

- **A comic book story** at the end of each chapter reviews instructional content while providing the basis for role-play and team tasks.

Downtown Components

Audio Tapes and CDs enhance learning through dialogues, listening practice, readings, and pronunciation exercises.

Workbooks reinforce lessons and maximize student practice of key reading, writing, listening, speaking, and grammar points.

Transparencies can be used to introduce lessons, develop vocabulary, and stimulate expansion activities.

Assessment CD-ROM with *ExamView® Pro* allows teachers to create, customize, and correct tests and quizzes quickly and easily.

Teacher's Editions with ArtBank CD-ROM provide student book answers and teaching suggestions.

Alignment with the CASAS, SCANS, EFF Competencies and state standards supports classroom and program goals.

Photo Credits

Chapter 1
Page 4, Royalty-Free/Corbis,
Page 4, Andersen/Ross/BrandX Pictures/Getty Images
Page 4, Jon Feingersh/CORBIS
Page 6, Nick Clements/ Getty Images
Page 6, Jose Luis Pelaez, Inc./CORBIS
Page 6, Chad Johnston/ Masterfile
Page 6, Mike Powell/Getty Images
P.2.01.08
Page 8, Masterfile
Page 8, Ted Wilcox / Index Stock Imagery
Page 9, Christina Micek
Page 9, Norbert Schaefer/CORBIS
Page 9, Pollok/ Getty Images
Page 11, Heads Up Headshots
Page 11, Scott Areman/CORBIS
Page 11, ThinkStock / SuperStock
Page 13, Royalty-Free/Corbis
Page 13, Dana White / Photo Edit
Page 13, Jon Riley / Index
P.2.01.21
Page 16, Thomas Craig / Index
Page 16, Anton Vengo / SuperStock
Page 16, Dana White/ Photo Edit
Page 16, Jeff Zaruba/CORBIS
Page 16, David Young-Wolff / Photo Edit

Chapter 2
Page 24, Tom Stewart/CORBIS
P.2.2.02
Page 24, Gary D. Landsman/CORBIS
Page 24, Scott Roper/CORBIS
Page 25, Jim McGuire / Index Stock Imagery
Page 25, David Young-Wolff / Photo Edit
Page 25, Peter Beck/CORBIS
Page 25, ThinkStock LLC / Index Stock Imagery
Page 39, Christina Micek
Page 39, Bonnie Kamin / Photo Edit
Page 39, G P Bowater / Alamy
Page 39, Bonnie Kamin / Index Stock Imagery

Chapter 3
Page 45, John Coletti
Page 45, Hemera Photo Objects
Page 45, Hemera Photo Objects
Page 45, Photodisc/ Getty Images
Page 45, Steven Mark Needham/Foodpix
Page 45, Hemera Photo Objects
Page 45, Hagiwara/ Foodpix
Page 46, Royalty-Free/Corbis
Page 46, Hemera Photo Objects
Page 46, Burke/Triolo Productions/ Foodpix
Page 46, Photodisc/ Getty Images
Page 46, Taesam Do/ Foodpix
Page 46, Christina Micek
Page 46, Christina Micek
Page 46, Christina Micek
Page 49, Hemera Photo Objects
Page 49, SuperStock, Inc. / SuperStock
Page 49, Hemera Photo Objects
Page 49, Richard Hutchings / Photo Edit
Page 49, Hemera Photo Objects
Page 53, Benelux Press / Index Stock Imagery

Chapter 4
Page 64, Tom Rosenthal / SuperStock
Page 64, Don Mason/CORBIS
Page 64, Penina/ Picture Arts
Page 64, Myrleen Ferguson Cate / Photo Edit
Page 69, David Binder
Page 69, Christina Micek
Page 69, Christina Micek
Page 69, Hemera Photo Objects
Page 69, Hemera Photo Objects

Chapter 5
Page 89, Digital Vision/ Getty Images
Page 89, Tom & Dee Ann McCarthy/CORBIS
Page 89, Christina Micek
Page 89, Masterfile Royalty Free Division
Page 94, LE SEGRETAIN PASCAL/CORBIS SYGMA
Page 94, Royalty-Free/Corbis
Page 94, Reuters/CORBIS
Page 94, Dan Lim/ Masterfile

Chapter 6
Page 106, Steve Chenn/CORBIS
P.2.6.02
Page 106, Royalty-Free/Corbis
Page 106, Tom Stewart/CORBIS
Page 113, Bonnie Kamin / Photo Edit

Chapter 7
Page 128, SuperStock, Inc. / SuperStock
Page 128, Christina Micek
Page 128, Christina Micek
Page 128, Dex Images, Inc./CORBIS
Page 130, Imagemore / SuperStock
Page 130, Tony Freeman / Photo Edit
Page 130, Royalty-Free/Corbis
Page 130, Sky Bonillo / Photo Edit

Chapter 8
Page 146, Pixtal / SuperStock
Page 146, Christina Kennedy / Photo Edit
Page 146, Ed Bock/CORBIS
Page 146, Christina Micek
Page 149, Colin Young-Wolff / Photo Edit
Page 149, David Pollack/CORBIS
Page 149, Michael Newman / Photo Edit
Page 149, Alan Schein Photography/CORBIS
Page 149, Royalty-Free/Corbis
Page 149, Ralf-Finn Hestoft/CORBIS
Page 152, Lester Lefkowitz/CORBIS

Chapter 9
Page 172, Bartomeu Amengual / Index Stock Imagery
Page 174, Stock Image / SuperStock
Page 174, Christina Micek
Page 174, Christina Micek
Page 174, Phil Banko/CORBIS
Chapter 10
Page 193, Royalty-Free/Corbis
P.2.10.2   Comstock/ Picture Quest
Page 193, Michael Newman / Photo Edit
Page 193, Michael Newman / Photo Edit
Page 193, AJA Productions/Getty Images

Personal Information

1 **Read** *Read the story. Match the numbers in the pictures to the words in the box.*

New in Town!

Jessica is a new student in Mr. Ryan's English class. She is from Colombia. Today is her first day in class. She is introducing herself to three other students. One of her classmates is from Russia. Her other classmates have different nationalities. Some are Mexican, Chinese, Vietnamese, and Spanish.

Jessica lives downtown with her uncle, aunt, and two cousins. She has a new job in her new town. She works in an office. She has a good work schedule and very nice coworkers. One is tall and thin, another is short and heavy. Jessica is talking about her hobby—something she likes to do in her free time. Jessica's supervisor is listening to the coworkers talk.

Jessica's family, classmates, and coworkers all look different. Some have blond hair, some have dark curly hair, and one is bald. Some are young and some are old. Some are her age. Jessica likes her new life downtown!

Listen 🎧

_____ a chalkboard
_____ a country
_____ a nationality
_____ an eraser
_____ a piece of chalk
_____ a pencil sharpener
_____ classmates
_____ a handshake
_____ uncle
_____ aunt
_____ bald
_____ cousins
_____ short gray hair
_____ blond hair
_____ dark curly hair
_____ hobby
_____ a work schedule
_____ a supervisor
_____ tall and thin
_____ short and heavy
_____ coworkers

Introductions

1 **Say It** Practice the conversation with a partner.

A: Hello. My name is <u>Jessica</u>.

B: Hi, <u>Jessica</u>. I'm <u>Tania</u>. Where are you from?

A: I'm <u>Colombian</u>. I'm from <u>Bogotá</u>. Where are you from?

B: I'm <u>Russian</u>. I'm from <u>Moscow</u>.

Tania / Russian / Moscow

Practice the conversation again. Use your name and the photographs below.

1. Ha / Chinese / Hong Kong

2. Luis / Mexican / Mexico City

3. Isabelle / French / Paris

2 **Write** Write the nationalities. Use complete sentences.

1. Jessica is from Colombia.   <u>She is Colombian</u>.

2. Manuel is from Mexico.   _____.

3. Hong Yu is from China.   _____.

4. Lin is from Vietnam.   _____.

5. I am from England.   _____.

6. Frank and Tony are from Italy.   _____.

3 **Group Practice** Work in groups of five or six. Introduce yourself to your classmates. Tell them your nationality and what city you are from. Then tell the teacher about one of your classmates.

Culture Tip

Handshakes

In business situations, it is polite to shake hands and smile when you meet someone. When do people shake hands in your country?

4 Write Look at the student registration form. Answer the questions about Manuel.

1. What's his last name?

   _____

2. Where does he live?

   _____

3. What's his zip code?

   _____

4. Where is he from?

   _____

5. When was he born?

   _____

STUDENT REGISTRATION FORM
FOR NEW AND RETURNING STUDENTS

LAST NAME: _Garcia_

FIRST NAME: _Manuel_

DATE: _9/7/05_

ADDRESS: _225 Main St._

CITY: _Los Angeles_

STATE: _CA_   ZIP CODE: _90013_

TELEPHONE: (_213_) _555-2346_

DATE OF BIRTH: _7/9/80_

PLACE OF BIRTH: _Mexico_

5 Listen Listen to the conversation between Hong Yu and the school counselor. Write the missing information in Hong Yu's student registration form.

STUDENT REGISTRATION FORM
FOR NEW AND RETURNING STUDENTS

LAST NAME: _____

FIRST NAME: _Hong Yu_

DATE: _September 21, 2005_

ADDRESS: _Spring St._

CITY: _Pasadena_

STATE: _CA_   ZIP CODE: _____

TELEPHONE: (____) _555-2987_

DATE OF BIRTH: ____/____/1982

PLACE OF BIRTH: _Hong Kong,_

6 Pair Practice Ask and answer questions about Hong Yu.

7 Pair Practice Exchange books with a partner. Ask questions to fill out the student registration form for your partner. Introduce your partner to another pair of students.

STUDENT REGISTRATION FORM
FOR NEW AND RETURNING STUDENTS

LAST NAME: _____

FIRST NAME: _____

DATE: _____

ADDRESS: _____

CITY: _____

STATE: _____   ZIP CODE: _____

TELEPHONE: (____) _____

DATE OF BIRTH: _____

PLACE OF BIRTH: _____

8 **Say It** Practice the conversation with a partner.

teacher / 5 years

A: What do you do?

B: I'm a student now, but I was <u>a teacher</u> in my country.

A: Really? How long were you <u>a teacher</u>?

B: I was <u>a teacher</u> for <u>five</u> years.

Practice the conversation again. Use the photographs below.

1. **lawyer / 6 years**

2. **accountant / 3 years**

3. **soccer player / 10 years**

GRAMMAR CHECK

Be: Past tense, *yes/no* questions and short answers

Pronoun	Positive	Negative
I/he/she/it	**was**	**wasn't (was not)**
we/you/they	**were**	**weren't (were not)**

Question	Positive Short Answer	Negative Short Answer
Were you a teacher in your country?	Yes, I **was**.	No, I **wasn't**.
Were they engineers?	Yes, they **were**.	No, they **weren't**.

Check Point:
✓ For negative short answers, use contractions.

9 **Write** Write statements and questions about the people in Activity 8. Read your statements and questions to a partner.

1. Dina/teacher   STATEMENT: <u>Dina was a teacher in her country</u> .

                    QUESTION: <u>Was Dina a teacher in her country</u> ?

2. Oscar/lawyer   STATEMENT: _____ .

                    QUESTION: _____ ?

3. Linh/accountant   STATEMENT: _____ .

                    QUESTION: _____ ?

4. Antonio/soccer player STATEMENT: _____ .

                    QUESTION: _____ ?

10 **Say It** Practice the conversation with a partner.

A: Was he born in Mexico?

B: Yes, he was.

A: Was he born in 1987?

B: No, he wasn't. He was born in 1978.

Mexico? 1987?

Practice the conversation again. Use the registration forms below.

1. China? 1978? 2. Russia? July? 3. Spain? August?

11 **Teamwork Task** Work in teams of five. Ask your teammates questions to complete the chart below.

Name	Nationality	Date of Birth	Job	Past Job

Introduce one of your teammates to the class. Give all of his or her information.

Game Time

When is your birthday?

One student will stand in front of the class. Ask *yes/no* questions to find out his or her birthday. Example: "Were you born in July?"

Family

1 **Say It** Practice the conversation with a partner.

**Uncle Roberto, Aunt Lupe,
cousins Martin and Dulce**

A: Let me introduce you to my family. This is my <u>uncle</u>. His name is <u>Roberto</u>.

B: Hello, <u>Roberto</u>.

A: This is my <u>aunt</u>. Her name is <u>Lupe</u>.

B: Hello, <u>Lupe</u>.

A: And these are my <u>cousins</u>. Their names are <u>Martin and Dulce</u>.

B: Nice to meet you, <u>Martin and Dulce</u>.

Practice the conversation again. Use the photographs below.

1. father: Bill, mother: Tuan, grandparents: Mr. and Mrs. Wang

2. brother: Pedro, sister-in-law: Jennifer, niece and nephew: Debbie and Ryan

2 **Pair Practice** Work with a partner. Fill out the chart for your partner. Ask the names and relationships of the people he or she lives with.

WHO DO YOU LIVE WITH?	
Name	**Relationship**

3 **Group Practice** Work in groups of four or five. Show a family photo, or draw a picture of three or four family members or friends. Introduce them to the people in your group.

Word Help: Hair

long & straight | short & curly with beard | wavy | blond
dark | gray | red | bald with mustache

4 **Say It** Practice the conversation with a partner.

my uncle and aunt

A: Who do you live with?

B: I live with my <u>uncle and aunt</u>. You know <u>them</u>, don't you?

A: I'm not sure. What <u>do they</u> look like?

B: <u>They're about 40 years old</u>. <u>My uncle is bald and has a mustache</u>. <u>My aunt has short gray hair</u>.

A: No, I don't think I know <u>them</u>.

Practice the conversation again. Use the photographs below.

1. wife

2. brother

3. parents

GRAMMAR CHECK

Object pronouns

Subject Pronoun	Object Pronoun	Example Sentences
I	**me**	I am with him. He is with **me**.
you	**you**	You called me. He called **you**.
he	**him**	He works with me. I work with **him**.
she	**her**	She found this gift. It is for **her**.
it	**it**	It is under the chair. Please pick **it** up.
we	**us**	We left at 11:00. That was late for **us**.
they	**them**	They are married. Give the gift to **them**.

Word Help: Height and weight

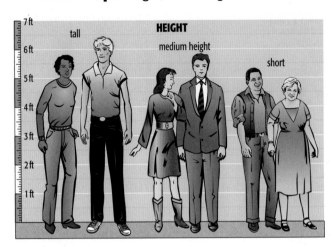

5 **Write** Describe the people in the pictures below. Write as much as you can.

_____ _____ _____

_____ _____ _____

_____ _____ _____

6 **Pair Practice** Work with a partner. Ask who he or she lives with. Ask your partner to describe them. Include age, height, weight, hair, etc.

Culture Tip

Age

In the U.S., it is not polite to ask someone how old they are, especially a teacher, supervisor, or someone older than you.

7 **Pair Practice** Work with a partner. Look through the pages of this book. Ask and answer questions about people in the book.

Example: *Student 1:* Does he have long hair?
Student 2: No, he doesn't.
Student 2: Is she thin?
Student 1: Yes, she is.

8 **Say It** Practice the conversation with a partner.

A: How tall is <u>Abel</u>?

B: He's <u>five foot nine</u>.

A: Is he tall or short?

B: He's <u>medium height</u>.

A: How much does he weigh?

B: He weighs <u>260 pounds</u>.

A: Is he thin or heavy?

B: He's <u>heavy</u>.

Use the two driver's licenses below to practice the conversation again.

9 **Teamwork Task** Work in teams of three or four. Look at Donna's driver's license below. Work together to write sentences about Donna. Write as many as you can. Then, create a character of your own. Will he or she be tall or short? Blond or dark? Young or old? Draw a driver's license and include the same information.

Game Time

Describe a famous person, such as an athlete, actor, or singer. Write as much as you can about the person. Include information such as height, weight, age, hair color, etc. Try to make your classmates guess who the person is.

First Day at Work

1 Read Jessica is taking a writing class at school. Her teacher asked the class to introduce themselves in an e-mail to their classmates.

Hello Classmates,

I received my H1 visa and I am working now at my new job in the United States. I work at the Downtown Animation Studio. Can you believe it? I am a computer animator. The job is very interesting. I am studying and learning about the software programs they use here.

My office is nice, and my supervisor is very smart. I have a beautiful new computer. I'm sure it was very expensive. I also have very friendly coworkers. I like my work schedule, too. I work four days a week, from Tuesday to Friday. I work from 8:00 a.m. to 7:00 p.m. That's ten hours of work and one hour for lunch.

So, my new job is great. Please write back and tell me how you are doing.

Take care,
Jessica

2 Write Read the sentences. Circle True or False.

1. Jessica has a new job.	True	False
2. Jessica is a computer programmer.	True	False
3. Jessica works at the Downtown Café.	True	False
4. Jessica likes her office.	True	False
5. Jessica works five days a week.	True	False
6. Jessica gets paid for her lunch hour.	True	False
7. Jessica has an expensive computer.	True	False
8. Jessica is writing to her friend.	True	False

3 **Say It** Practice the conversation with a partner.

Where are the rest rooms?

A: Is this your first day on the job?

B: Yes, it is.

A: Is there anything I can help you with? Do you have any questions?

B: Maybe just one.

A: OK, sure.

B: <u>Where are the rest rooms?</u>

Practice the conversation again. Use the pictures to practice below.

1. **Who is the supervisor?**

2. **What time is the lunch break?**

3. **When do we get paid?**

GRAMMAR CHECK

Wh- question words

	Wh- word			Example
Use	**who**	for a	person.	**Who** are you looking for?
Use	**what**	for a	thing.	**What** do you want?
Use	**where**	for a	place.	**Where** are we meeting?
Use	**when**	for a	time.	**When** do you leave on vacation?
Use	**why**	for a	reason.	**Why** do you want to know?

4 **Write** Write the correct *wh-* question words.

1. _____ does Jessica work?   At the Downtown Animation Studio.

2. _____ is she writing to?   Her classmates.

3. _____ is her job title?   She is a computer animator.

4. _____ does she finish work?   At 7:00 P.M.

5. _____ does she like her job?   Because it's very interesting.

⑤ Pair Practice Ask and answer the questions about Mr. Ryan's work schedule.

WORK SCHEDULE: Mr. Eric Ryan		
	Monday–Thursday	**Friday**
8:00–10:00	English 1–Room 33	Meet with teachers
10:00–12:00	English 2–Room 30	
12:00–1:00	Lunch–Cafeteria	
1:00–3:00	Counseling–Library	

1. When does Mr. Ryan start work?
2. What does he teach at 8:00?
3. Where does he teach at 10:00?
4. Who does he meet with on Friday?
5. Where is he from 12:00 to 1:00?
6. When does he work in the library?

Ask more questions about Mr. Ryan's work schedule. Ask as many as you can.

⑥ Write Read the statements. Change the statements to questions.

1. Jessica works <u>in an office</u>.   <u>Where does Jessica work</u>?
2. Mr. Ryan teaches <u>from Monday to Thursday</u>.   _____?
3. Ms. Lemonis teaches <u>in Room 19</u>.   _____?
4. <u>Mr. Jones</u> teaches English 1.   _____?
5. Miss Green teaches <u>English 3</u>.   _____?
6. Jessica is happy <u>because she loves her job</u>. _____?

⑦ Write Write six questions for a new coworker or classmate. Use the question words below.

1. Who . . . _____?
2. What . . . _____?
3. Where . . . _____?
4. When . . . _____?
5. Why . . . _____?
6. What . . . _____?

⑧ Pair Practice Ask a classmate your six questions. Answer his or her six questions. Share his or her six answers with another pair or with the class, or role-play the interview in front of the class.

9 **Say It** Practice the conversation with a partner.

ski / dance

A: What do you like to do on the weekends?

B: I like to <u>ski</u>. How about you?

A: I like to <u>dance</u> on the weekends.

B: Oh, that's a great hobby.

Practice the conversation again. Use the pictures below.

1. **go hiking / play tennis**   2. **paint / go to museums**

10 **Group Practice** Work with a large group or the whole class. First write *yes/no* questions for each of the statements below. Then ask other students the questions. If a student says "Yes," write his or her name on the line in the STATEMENT column. If he or she says "No," ask another question.

Find someone who . . .

	STATEMENT	QUESTION	
1.	_____ likes to swim.	<u>Do you like to swim</u>	?
2.	_____ likes to dance.	_____	?
3.	_____ likes to go to museums.	_____	?
4.	_____ likes to paint or draw.	_____	?
5.	_____ likes to watch soccer games.	_____	?
6.	_____ likes to play baseball.	_____	?

11 Listen Listen to the conversations. Write the correct words under each picture. Use these phrases: *watch TV, read books, go to the movies, jog, play cards,* and *bake.*

_____

_____

_____

_____

_____

_____

12 Pair Practice Work with a partner. Ask and answer questions about the hobbies in Activity 11. Then tell your classmates what your partner likes and doesn't like to do.

13 Teamwork Task Work in teams of three or four. Choose one student as the team writer. Your teacher will give you a five-minute time limit. Work together to brainstorm two lists: a list of hobbies and a list of jobs. Write the hobbies and jobs on the lines below.

HOBBIES

_____

_____

_____

_____

_____

JOBS

_____

_____

_____

_____

_____

Homework

Interview someone outside the class, asking them questions about their daily schedule, job, and their hobbies. You may wish to start with the six questions you wrote in Activity 7 on page 14. Share your interview with the class.

1 **Read and Listen** Read the story. Then listen to the story.

New in Town

Jessica is twenty-four years old and new in town. She was born in Colombia, South America, but she lives in the United States now. She lives in Los Angeles, California. In her new home, she lives with her uncle, her aunt, and her two cousins. She doesn't know them well, but she likes them very much.

In Colombia, Jessica was an artist, but the pay wasn't very good. Now she is a computer animator and the pay is very good. She misses her parents and her brother and sister, but she is excited about her new life in the U.S. She also has a new school where she is studying English. She has some very interesting classmates. One is Russian. She was a dancer in her country. Another is Italian. He was a soccer player in his country for ten years.

Jessica has a lot of hobbies. She likes to ski in the winter and she likes to hike in the summer. She also likes to ride her bicycle and dance. But she doesn't have much free time for hobbies right now. For now, her job is her hobby!

2 **Write** Write answers to the questions in complete sentences.

1. What is the name of Jessica's native country? _____ .
2. Where is her native country? _____ .
3. Who does she miss? _____ .
4. What was her job in Colombia? _____ .
5. What does she do now? _____ .
6. How is her pay now? _____ .
7. How old is Jessica? _____ .
8. Who does she live with? _____ .
9. What are Jessica's hobbies? _____ .

CRITICAL THINKING:
10. Is Jessica a smart young woman? Why or why not?

    _____

3 **Write** Write an e-mail to Jessica. Tell her where you are from and where you live now. Tell her who you live with. Tell her about your hobbies. Tell her what you do now and what you want to do in the future.

4 **Best Answer** Bubble the correct answer.

                                                                             a   b   c

1. My father's brother is my _____.
   a) uncle   b) aunt   c) cousin   ◯ ◯ ◯

2. My _____ is the hours I work.
   a) supervisor   b) coworker   c) work schedule   ◯ ◯ ◯

3. What do you do?
   a) I'm a teacher. b) Fine, thank you. c) My job.   ◯ ◯ ◯

4. When does he work?
   a) Downtown.   b) He's a lawyer.   c) From 8:00 to 4:00. ◯ ◯ ◯

5. Do you have any hobbies?
   a) I have a car.   b) I'm a doctor.   c) I like to play tennis. ◯ ◯ ◯

5 **Write** Write these words on the correct lines below: *a hobby, a nationality, a grandfather, a job, a workplace, a work schedule, a height,* and *a weight.*

_____

_____

_____

_____

MEXICAN

_____

_____

_____

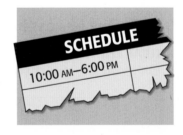

_____

6 **Write** Complete the dialogue below with your information.

A: Welcome to the Downtown English School. I'm glad you want to learn English.

B: Thank you.

A: I need to ask you some questions. First, when is your birthday?

B: _____ .

A: And where are you from?

B: _____ .

(give nationality and city)

A: Were you a teacher in your country?

B: No, _____ .

A: What do you do now?

B: _____ .

A: What is your work schedule?

B: _____ .

A: And one last question. Do you have any hobbies?

B: Yes. _____ .

7 **Pair Practice** Practice the conversation in Activity 6 with a partner.

8 **Teamwork Task** Work in teams of four. Complete the Class Information Chart for yourself and your teammates. Student 1: Ask name and nationality. Student 2: Ask address and jobs. Student 3: Ask height and hair color. Student 4: Ask about hobbies. Share your information with the class.

Class Information Chart

	Student 1	Student 2	Student 3	Student 4
Name				
Nationality				
Address				
Current job				
Past job				
Height				
Hair color				
Hobbies				

PRONUNCIATION *Wh-* question intonation

A. Your voice goes up at the end of *yes/no* questions.

Do you know him?   Is he thin?

At the end of a *wh-* question, your voice goes up a little and then down.

What do you want?   Who are you looking for?

B. Listen and draw the arrow. Listen again and repeat.

What do you want?   When do you leave on vacation?

Who are you looking for?   Why do you want to know?

Where are we meeting?   How long were you a teacher?

INTERNET IDEA

Search the Internet for information about your native country. Where is it located? How big is it? What language is spoken there? How many people live there? What kinds of jobs do people have? Tell your class about your country. Bring in photos or pictures.

I can . . .			
• identify countries and nationalities.	1	2	3
• give personal information.	1	2	3
• talk about present and past jobs.	1	2	3
• complete a student registration form.	1	2	3
• describe family members and people you know.	1	2	3
• talk about height and weight.	1	2	3
• talk about work schedules.	1	2	3
• talk about hobbies.	1	2	3
• use the past tense of *be*.	1	2	3
• use *wh-* question words.	1	2	3

1 = not well   2 = OK   3 = very well

9 **Write** Write the missing words in the cartoon story. Use these words: *parents, brother, niece, nephew, sister-in-law, was, were, What, them, family, you,* and *Mexican.*

Alberto: Cindy, I'd like to introduce you to my (1)_____. These are my (2)_____, José and Berta Gonzalez.

Cindy: Nice to meet you, Mr. and Mrs. Gonzales.
Alberto: My dad is retired now, but he (3)_____ a doctor.

Alberto: This is my (4)_____, Oscar. And this is my (5)_____, Lupe. And these two are my (6)_____ and (7)_____.

Alberto: Oscar is (8)_____. But Lupe was born in California.
Cindy: Really? (9)_____ city in California?

Lupe: Los Angeles.
Cindy: Me, too. Maybe we (10)_____ neighbors!

Cindy: You have a very big family, Alberto.
Alberto: Yes, and they all like (11)_____ very much.
Cindy: I'm glad. I like (12)_____, too.

10 **Group Practice** Work in groups of three. Practice the story.

Daily Activities

GOALS

✓ Identify household chores

✓ Talk about frequency of activities

✓ Use *make* and *do* expressions

✓ Read a map

✓ Use *can* and *could* for possibility

✓ Distinguish between current and habitual actions

✓ Understand a postal delivery schedule

✓ Understand postal rates and services

✓ Talk about your commute

1 **Read** *Read the story. Match the numbers in the pictures to the words in the box.*

Chores and Duties

Jessica doesn't pay rent at her aunt and uncle's house, but she does help them do their household chores. She cooks dinner three nights a week. She washes dishes on days when she doesn't cook. She does some of the laundry and waters the garden occasionally. She pays some of the bills. And of course she makes her bed every morning.

Several of Jessica's friends and classmates work in her neighborhood. Her friend, Tania, is a salesperson in a small clothing store. Her friend, Vida, is a hairstylist. And Cindy works in a café. She makes coffee for eight hours a day. And she drinks a lot of coffee, too!

Listen 🎧

_____ cooking
_____ delivering mail
_____ washing dishes
_____ cutting hair
_____ doing laundry
_____ making a bed
_____ paying bills
_____ watering the garden
_____ a café
_____ a hair salon
_____ a clothing store
_____ a hairstylist
_____ a salesperson
_____ a customer
_____ letters
_____ a package
_____ priority mail
_____ making coffee

What's She Doing?

1 **Say It** Practice the conversation with a partner.

every morning

A: What <u>is she</u> doing?
B: <u>She is making the bed</u>.
A: How often <u>does she make the bed</u>?
B: <u>She makes the bed every morning</u>.

Practice the conversation again. Use the pictures below.

1. once a month   2. twice a week   3. every weekend

GRAMMAR CHECK

How often questions and answers

once = one time   *twice* = two times

Put frequency time expressions at the end of the sentence:

How often do you cook dinner?   I cook dinner **once a week.**
How often do you call your mother?   I call her **every day.**

2 **Write** Answer the questions with true information about you.

1. How often do you cook dinner? _____ .

2. How often do you wash your windows? _____ .

3. How often do you vacuum your living room? _____ .

4. How often do you do your laundry? _____ .

5. How often do you clean your room? _____ .

3 **Group Practice** Work in groups of four or five. Ask your group members how often they do household chores. Start with the chores in Activity 2. Then ask about other chores, duties, or activities.

Word Help: *make* vs. *do*

There are many expressions that use *make* or *do*, but only one of these verbs is correct in each expression.

We say **make the beds**, not **do the beds**.

We say **do the dishes**, not **make the dishes**.

4 **Write** Write *make* or *do* with each of the expressions below.

1. _____ the laundry
2. _____ breakfast
3. _____ the shopping
4. _____ your homework
5. _____ a cake

6. _____ exercises
7. _____ the housework
8. _____ a phone call
9. _____ the beds
10. _____ the dishes

5 **Listen** Listen to the conversation. Correct any mistakes in Activity 4.

6 **Say It** Practice the conversation with a partner.

my husband

A: Who usually <u>does the dishes</u> in your home?

B: <u>My husband usually does the dishes in my home.</u> How about in your home?

A: _____ usually <u>do/does the dishes in my home</u>.

Practice the conversation again. Use the pictures below.

1. my daughter

2. my grandmother

3. my parents

Frequency words

◄ 0% ──────────┼──────────┼────────── 50% ──────────┼──────────┼────────── 100% ►
never   rarely   seldom   sometimes   often   usually   always

We use frequency words *before* most verbs in a sentence:
I **always wash** the dishes.

With the verb *to be*, we use frequency words *after* the verb:
I **am always** asleep by 10:00.

7 **Write** Complete the sentences with a frequency word that makes the sentence true for you.

1. I _____ do the dishes in my home.

2. I _____ make dinner for myself or my family.

3. I _____ make my own bed.

4. I _____ clean the bathroom in my home.

5. I _____ do the grocery shopping for myself or my family.

6. I _____ do exercises.

7. I _____ help my children with their homework.

8. I am _____ late for class.

8 **Pair Practice** Work with a partner. Ask your partner *How often* questions about the chores in Activity 7.

Example: *How often do you wash the dishes in your home?*

9 **Write** Write five sentences about your partner using frequency words.

_____

_____

_____

_____

_____

Note: *Housework* or *household chores* are any activities that have to be done regularly in a home. They include cooking, cleaning, taking care of children or pets, paying bills, making small repairs, or any other activities that are necessary to maintain a home.

10 **Group Practice** Work in a large group or with the whole class. First write *How often* questions for the statements below. Then ask other students the questions. If a student answers with the same frequency word as below, write his or her name on the line.

Find someone who . . .

STATEMENT	QUESTION
1. _____ always washes the dishes.	How often . . . _____ ?
2. _____ usually makes dinner.	_____ ?
3. _____ pays bills.	_____ ?
4. _____ makes repairs.	_____ ?
5. _____ never helps children with homework.	_____ ?

11 **Teamwork Task** Work in teams of three. Make a list of ten household chores. Ask your teammates how often they do each one. Fill out the chart with frequency words for yourself and your two teammates.

HOUSEHOLD CHORE	STUDENT 1	STUDENT 2	STUDENT 3
1.			
2.			
3.			
4.			
5.			
6.			
7.			
8.			
9.			
10.			

Game Time

Your teacher will think of a household chore he or she doesn't like to do. Guess what it is by asking yes/no questions. Continue the game with your classmates.

Jessica's Neighborhood

Lesson 2

1 **Listen** Listen to the conversations. Write the names of the places you hear on the map below.

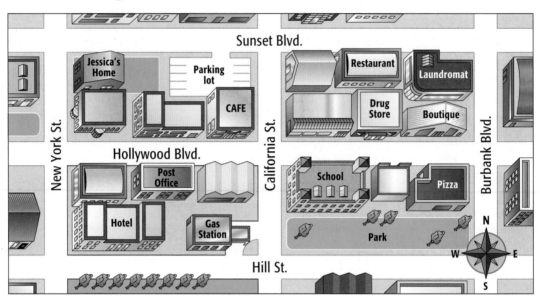

2 **Write** Look at the map. Answer the questions.

1. What direction does Hill Street run? _____ .
2. What part of the map represents the north? (Top? Bottom? Left? Right?)
   _____ .
3. What direction does California Street run? _____ .
4. What part of the map represents the east? _____ .
5. Find the intersection of California Street and Hollywood Boulevard. What is on the northeast corner of the intersection? _____ .
6. What is on the southeast corner of California Street and Hollywood Boulevard? _____ .

3 **Pair Practice** Work with a partner. Ask and answer questions about Jessica's neighborhood.

Example: *Student 1:* Where is the post office?
Student 2: It's on Hollywood Boulevard next to the health club.

Note: Use prepositions of location such as **next to, between, across from,** and **on the corner of** to help you describe locations.

GRAMMAR
CHECK

Simple present: Habitual actions

Subject	Verb	*How often*
I/You/We/They	**cook**	every day. every morning. every Sunday.
He/She/It	**cooks**	once a week. twice a week. once a month. twice a month.

Checkpoints:
- ✓ Use the **simple present** to talk about things you do regularly or habitually. Jessica **feeds** the ducks **every Sunday**.
- ✓ Use the present continuous to talk about something that is happening now. Use the correct form of *be* + **verb** + *ing*. Jessica **is feeding** the ducks now.

4 **Say It** Practice the conversation with a partner.

every Sunday

A: Where is Jessica?

B: She's <u>at the park</u>.

A: What's she doing?

B: She<u>'s feeding the ducks</u>. She <u>feeds the ducks every Sunday at the park</u>.

Practice the conversation again. Use the pictures below.

1. 3 times a week   2. every weeknight   3. every weekend

5 **Write** Write about your habits. What are some things you do regularly? How often do you do them? Are they good habits or bad habits?

WHAT?	HOW OFTEN?	GOOD or BAD	SENTENCE
a shower	every morning	good	I take a shower every morning.

6 **Pair Practice** Read your habits from Activity 5 to a partner. Then have your partner describe your habits to another pair of students.

GRAMMAR CHECK

Can for ability

Use *can* to show ability. *Can* shows that you are able to do something, or it is possible to do something.
You **can** buy ice cream at the supermarket = You **are able to** buy ice cream at the supermarket.

7 **Pair Practice** Match the activities in Column B with the places in Column A. Discuss the vocabulary with your partner.

A	B
_____ 1. supermarket	**a.** mail a letter
_____ 2. hair salon	**b.** buy groceries
_____ 3. bank	**c.** exercise
_____ 4. post office	**d.** get a haircut
_____ 5. health club	**e.** fill a prescription
_____ 6. drugstore/pharmacy	**f.** cash a check

8 **Write** Write six sentences about the places in Activity 7.

1. <u>You can buy groceries at the supermarket</u>   .
2. _____ .
3. _____ .
4. _____ .
5. _____ .
6. _____ .

9 **Say It** Practice the conversation with a partner.

jogging / swimming

A: Where is Jessica?

B: She's at the <u>health club</u>.

A: What's she doing there?

B: I'm not sure. She could be <u>jogging</u> or she could be <u>swimming</u>.

A: I think she's probably <u>swimming</u>.

B: Yes, you're probably right.

Practice the conversation again. Use the pictures below.

1. **filling a prescription / buying shampoo**

2. **mailing a letter / buying some stamps**

3. **cashing a check / depositing some money**

> **Note:** *could* and ***probably***
>
> Use *could* for possibility (when you are less than 50% sure about something).
>
> She **could** be at the café. (It is possible that she is at the café, but she could be somewhere else, too.)
>
> Use *probably* when you are more than 50% sure about something, but less than 100% sure.
>
> She is at the post office; she is **probably** mailing a letter.

10 **Teamwork Task** Work in teams of three or four. Make a list of stores or other business places in your neighborhood or town. Write what you *can do* in each one. Write as many places as you can. Draw a map of these places.

PLACE	WHAT YOU CAN DO THERE

Game Time

Play this game in groups of five or six.
1. Write the name of a place in your neighborhood on a piece of paper.
2. Write something you can do in that place.
3. Pretend you are there right now.
4. Ask other students in your group yes/no questions to find out where they are and what they are doing.

Example: Student 1: Are you in the supermarket?
Student 2: Yes, I am.
Student 3: Are you buying groceries?

What Do You Do at Work?

1 Read Jessica's teacher asked the class to interview people in their neighborhood about their jobs. Read Robert's e-mail. Discuss the vocabulary in the box.

Hi Jessica,

Thanks for asking me to describe my job for your English class. I'll tell you about my job. I am your mail carrier. I deliver the mail in your neighborhood. But there are some things you probably don't know about my job. For one thing, I arrive at work at 6:45 every morning. That's hard for me because I live in the suburbs, far away from downtown, and I commute to work. It takes me an hour to get to work. When I arrive, I sort the mail for an hour. Then I go out on my route. (That's the area where I deliver the mail.) I have a schedule I always follow. For example, first I walk up California Street between 9:00 and 10:00. Then I pick up another sack of mail and walk down Burbank Boulevard between 10:15 and 11:15. The job has good benefits. One important benefit is that it keeps me healthy. I get a lot of exercise every day!

Your new e-mail pal,
Robert

suburbs	sack
commute	benefits
route	

2 Write Read the sentences. Circle True or False.

1.	Robert is a mail clerk.	True	False
2.	Robert works in Jessica's neighborhood.	True	False
3.	Robert lives in Jessica's neighborhood.	True	False
4.	Robert gets up at 5:45 every morning.	True	False
5.	Robert commutes an hour each way.	True	False
6.	Robert follows a schedule.	True	False
7.	Robert is walking on California Street at 10:30.	True	False
8.	Robert is delivering mail on Burbank Boulevard at 11:00.	True	False

Note: Use the **simple present tense** for regularly scheduled events.
The train **leaves** every morning at 8:00.
The museum **opens** at 10:30 on Mondays.

ROUTE 4 – Mail Delivery Schedule	
9:00–10:00 California Street	**12:50–2:30** Orange Street
10:15–11:15 Burbank Boulevard	**2:35–3:00** Pine Street
11:20–11:45 New York Avenue	**3:10** Return to post office
11:45–12:15 Lunch	**3:15** Leave work
12:20–12:45 Apple Street	

3 **Pair Practice** Work with a partner. Use Robert's delivery schedule to ask and answer the questions below.

1. When does Robert leave work every day?

2. When does he eat lunch?

3. When does Robert deliver mail on Pine Street?

4. When do people on Orange Street get their mail?

5. When does the mail arrive on New York Avenue?

6. When does Robert return to the post office?

7. When does Robert arrive on Apple Street?

Ask and answer three more questions about Robert's delivery schedule.

4 **Write** Make a list of things you do on a regular schedule on a piece of paper. (For example, *I arrive at English class at 8:15.*) Add other things you know that have a regular schedule. (For example, *English class begins at 8:30.*) Write as many things about your life as you can. Use the schedule below to write your schedule for one day of your week.

My Schedule

7:00		**3:00**	
8:00		**4:00**	
9:00		**5:00**	
10:00		**6:00**	
11:00		**7:00**	
12:00		**8:00**	
1:00		**9:00**	
2:00		**10:00**	

5 **Say It** Practice the conversation with a partner.

A: I'd like to send this to <u>Santa Monica</u>.

B: How would you like to send it?

A: By <u>priority mail</u>, I think. How long does that take?

B: It takes <u>one to two days</u>. Is that OK?

A: Yes, that's fine.

Santa Monica / 1–2 days

Practice the conversation again. Use the pictures below.

1. **Miami / 1 day**

2. **New York / 1–2 weeks**

3. **Austin / 2–3 days**

POSTAL RATE CHART			
FIRST CLASS MAIL	**PRIORITY MAIL**	**BOOK RATE**	**EXPRESS MAIL**
Up to 1 oz. = $.37 2 oz. = $.60 3 oz. = $.83 4 oz. = $1.06	Up to 1 lb. = $3.85 2 lb. = $3.95 3 lb. = $4.75 4 lb. = $5.30	Up to 1 lb. = $1.42 2 lb. = $1.84 3 lb. = $2.26 4 lb. = $2.68	Up to 8 oz. = $13.65 2 lb. = $17.85 3 lb. = $21.05 4 lb. = $24.20

> **Note: Ounces and Pounds**
> **Oz.** is the abbreviation for ounces.
> **Lb.** is the abbreviation for pounds.
> 16 ounces = 1 pound

6 **Pair Practice** Use the pictures and the postal rate chart to practice conversations with a partner. Follow the example.

A: I'd like to send this by <u>express mail</u>.

B: OK.

A: How much does it cost?

B: Let's see. How much does it weigh?

A: It weighs <u>ten ounces</u>.

B: Then it costs <u>$17.85</u>.

7 Write Look at the pictures below. What are the people doing? What do they do at work every day?

WHAT ARE THEY DOING NOW?

Cindy is making coffee.

_____

_____

_____

WHAT DO THEY DO EVERY DAY AT WORK?

She makes coffee every day.

_____

_____

_____

GRAMMAR CHECK

Nonaction verbs

Some verbs don't use the present continuous tense when the time is now; they always use the simple present.

How much does it **weigh**? It **weighs** two pounds.
Not: How much is it *weighing*? It is *weighing* two pounds.

Check Point:
✓ Some other common nonaction verbs are *want, need, like, love, have, know, understand, see, hear, cost,* and *believe.*

8 Write Circle the correct form of the verb in the sentences below.

1. I (want / am wanting) to mail this package.

2. She (knows / is knowing) him very well.

3. The teacher (teaches / is teaching) a lesson right now.

4. She doesn't have a pencil. She (needs / is needing) one.

5. I (listen / am listening) to the teacher right now.

6. I (believe / am believing) you.

7. What are you doing? I (cook / am cooking) dinner.

8. What's in the closet? I (see / am seeing) some books and pencils.

9. How much is it? It (costs / is costing) $25.

10. What's she doing? She (studies / is studying) English.

9 **Say It** Practice the conversation with a partner.

Jessica / 45 minutes

A: <u>Does Jessica</u> work in <u>her</u> neighborhood?

B: No, <u>she doesn't. She works downtown</u>.

A: How long is <u>her</u> commute?

B: Pardon?

A: How long does it take <u>her</u> to get to work?

B: Oh. It takes <u>her</u> about <u>forty-five minutes</u>.

Practice the conversation again. Use the pictures below.

1. Lin / 35 minutes

2. Roberto / an hour

3. Mr. and Mrs. Chung / 20 minutes

Note: Your *commute* is the distance from your home to your school or job.

10 **Teamwork Task** Work in teams of four. Fill out the chart below about your teammates. Follow the example.

NAME	Jessica			
LOCATION OF HOME	Los Angeles			
LOCATION OF WORK OR SCHOOL	downtown			
HOW DOES HE OR SHE COMMUTE?	by car			
LENGTH OF COMMUTE	45 minutes			

Tell the class about your teammates.

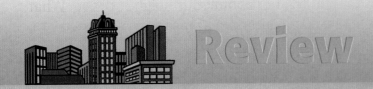

1 **Read and Listen** Read the story. Then listen to the story.

Jessica's New Neighborhood

Jessica's home life in the United States is not very different from her life at home in Colombia. The housework is the same. She does most of the same household chores. The biggest difference is that in Colombia, Jessica's mother did the laundry and cooked for the whole family.

But Jessica's new neighborhood is very different. There are many stores, restaurants, and businesses she can walk to in her neighborhood. She could eat a different kind of food every day if she had the money! There is a Japanese restaurant across the street, a café right next door, a pizza shop, a Chinese restaurant, and a supermarket nearby. There is also a hotel with an American restaurant inside. Jessica sometimes thinks that Americans like to eat, but they don't often like to cook.

A lot of Jessica's friends and classmates work in her neighborhood. Her friend Vida cuts hair in the hair salon. Tania sells clothes in a small boutique. Cindy works in a coffee shop or café. And Rosa is a personal trainer in the health club.

Some of Jessica's neighbors go to the health club. They exercise there three or four times a week. Maybe they have to exercise a lot because there are so many restaurants nearby!

2 **Write** Answer the questions below.

1. Who did Jessica's laundry in Colombia? _____

2. How is Jessica's home life in Colombia similar to her life in the United States?

_____

3. What kind of restaurant is next door to Jessica's home? _____

4. Where can you buy food in Jessica's neighborhood? _____

_____

5. Vida is at work. What is she probably doing? _____

6. Where does Rosa work? _____

7. Why do Jessica's neighbors exercise often? _____

CRITICAL THINKING:

8. Is your neighborhood like Jessica's? Why or why not? _____

_____

3 **Write** Write an e-mail to Jessica. Tell her about your neighborhood. What stores, restaurants, or businesses are in your neighborhood? What can you buy or eat there? Write as much as you can.

4 **Best Answer** Bubble the correct answer.

               a   **b**

1. What's she doing?
   a) She washes dishes.   b) She's washing dishes.   ◯   ◯

2. What's he doing?
   a) He's doing repairs.   b) He's making repairs.   ◯   ◯

3. What direction does Main Street run?
   a) north and west   b) east and west   ◯   ◯

4. What can you do at the hair salon?
   a) You can to get a haircut.   b) You can get a haircut.   ◯   ◯

5. I want it to arrive tomorrow.
   a) Send it by book rate.   b) Send it by express mail.   ◯   ◯

5 **Say It** Practice the conversation with a partner.

A: What is <u>she</u> doing?
B: <u>She's making coffee</u>.
A: How often does <u>she make coffee</u>?
B: <u>She makes coffee about ten times a day</u>.

10 times a day

Practice the conversation three more times. Use the pictures below.

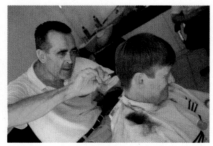

1. **5 times a week**   2. **20 times a day**   3. **every morning**

6 Teamwork Task Make a list of jobs in your neighborhood or school. Interview people that work at those jobs. Fill in the chart below.

NAME OF PERSON AND JOB	JOB DESCRIPTION	COMMUTE

Pronunciation Present tense *s* endings

Present tense verbs that follow *he, she,* and *it* end in the letter *s*. However, this *s* ending has three different pronunciations. It can sound like *s, z,* or *iz*.

A. Listen and repeat these sentences. Listen to the *s* ending.

Sounds like *s*	She cooks dinner.
Sounds like *z*	She pays the bills.
Sounds like *iz*	She washes the dishes.

B. You will hear nine verbs. Listen for the *s* endings. Write each verb in the correct column.

Sounds like *s*	**Sounds like *z***	**Sounds like *iz***
makes	_____	_____
_____	_____	_____
_____	_____	_____

INTERNET IDEA

Using a map service on the Internet, enter your home address as your starting address and your school as your destination. Print out the map and bring it to class. Use it to describe your commute to your classmates.

I can . . .			
• identify household chores.	1	2	3
• talk about frequency of activities.	1	2	3
• use *make* and *do* expressions.	1	2	3
• read a map.	1	2	3
• use *can* and *could* for possibility.	1	2	3
• distinguish between current and habitual actions.	1	2	3
• understand a postal delivery schedule.	1	2	3
• understand postal rates and services.	1	2	3
• talk about your commute.	1	2	3

1 = not well   2 = OK   3 = very well

7 **Write** Write the missing words in the cartoon story. Use these words: *pay, housework, could, make, do* (5), *wash, to clean, twice, chores* (2).

Cindy: When we get married, Alberto, I'm not going to do all the (1)_____.
Alberto: I know Cindy. I understand that.

Cindy: What (2)_____ are you going to do?
Alberto: I like to cook and wash my car.

Cindy: OK. You can cook (3)_____ a week. On the days that you cook, I'll (4)_____ the dishes.
Alberto: That sounds OK.

Cindy: I don't like (5)_____.
Alberto: Nobody likes cleaning, Cindy.
Cindy: I'll (6)_____ the laundry if you clean the bathroom.

Alberto: And I'll (7)_____ the bed if you (8)_____ all the bills.
Cindy: Sure, I'd like to (9)_____ that.
Alberto: And why don't we (10)_____ the shopping together?
Cindy: Yes, we (11)_____ do that.

Cindy: Why don't we (12)_____ everything 50/50?
Alberto: OK. We both work, so that's fair.
Cindy: This is a big change from the way our parents (13)_____ their (14)_____.
Alberto: Yes, it is!

8 **Pair Practice** Practice the story with a partner.

Chapter 2 Review **41**

Food

GOALS

✓ Identify places in the kitchen

✓ Identify common Thanksgiving foods

✓ Identify common beverages

✓ Distinguish between count and noncount nouns

✓ Interpret food labels

✓ Give and take restaurant orders

✓ Read ads and coupons

✓ Write a shopping list

✓ Work together to plan a party

1 **Read** *Read the story. Match the numbers in the pictures to the words in the box.*

Thanksgiving Dinner

It is the fourth Thursday in November and Jessica's family is going to have a big Thanksgiving dinner. They are going to share Thanksgiving dinner with some friends and neighbors and two of Jessica's classmates.

Jessica is going to set the table with dishes and silverware—spoons, forks and knives—and she is going to light two candles. Then they are going to eat turkey and stuffing with two kinds of potatoes: mashed potatoes and sweet potatoes. They are also going to have corn and a salad. Jessica's classmates are going to bring dessert. For dessert they are going to have ice cream, pie, and cookies. They are going to have coffee and tea, too. Jessica thinks it's going to be a very delicious Thanksgiving dinner!

Listen 🎧

____ napkins
____ cabinet
____ salad
____ kitchen table
____ refrigerator
____ counter
____ freezer
____ stuffing
____ silverware
____ apple pie
____ glasses
____ mashed potatoes
____ ice cream
____ cheese
____ coffee
____ tea
____ sweet potatoes
____ milk
____ corn
____ dishes
____ bread
____ soda
____ candles
____ turkey
____ cookies
____ plates
____ bowls
____ ice
____ butter

Thanksgiving Dinner

Culture Tip

Thanksgiving

Thanksgiving is a traditional U. S. holiday. It is the fourth Thursday of November. What traditional holidays do you celebrate? Describe these holidays.

1 **Say It** Practice the conversation with a partner.

corn? candles?

A: Is there any <u>corn</u> in the kitchen?

B: Yes, there is.

A: Where is it?

B: It's <u>on the counter</u>.

A: Are there any <u>candles</u> in the kitchen?

B: Yes, there are.

A: Where are they?

B: They are <u>behind the salad</u>.

Practice the conversation again. Use the pictures below.

1. silverware? napkins?

2. coffee? dishes?

3. soda? cookies?

GRAMMAR CHECK

Count and noncount nouns

Most nouns are count nouns. They have singular and plural forms.
   one plate, two plates; one apple, two apples

Some nouns are noncount. They don't have separate parts (like bread or cake) or the parts are very small (like salt or sugar). These nouns have only one form.
   I'd like **some** bread. (*Not* a bread or two breads).

Check Point:
   ✓ Some examples of noncount food nouns are *fruit, rice, salt, pepper, sugar, garlic, soup, oil, lettuce, meat,* and *butter*.

2 Write
Look at the picture on pages 42–43. Make a list of all the nouns you see in Jessica's kitchen. Put them in the correct column: **count** or **noncount**.

COUNT		NONCOUNT
cookies		ice

3 Pair Practice
Work with a partner. Ask about the foods below.

Example: *Student 1:* Is there any ice cream in your kitchen right now?
Student 2: Yes, there is. (*or* No, there isn't.)
Student 1: Are there any apples in your kitchen right now?
Student 2: Yes, there are. (*or* No, there aren't.)

1   2   3   4

5   6   7   8

Note: Containers

Sometimes we use noncount nouns in the plural form, but it is the containers or packages we are counting, not the food itself.

Example: "I'd like two sugars" might mean two *packets* of sugar or two *spoons* of sugar, but **not** really two sugars.

Example: "I'd like two sodas," might mean two *cans* of soda, or two *glasses* of soda, but **not** really two sodas.

④ Match Match the food below with its most common container.

_____ **1.** oil   **a.** bag
_____ **2.** honey   **b.** box
_____ **3.** rice   **c.** can
_____ **4.** soup   **d.** jar
_____ **5.** chips   **e.** pint
_____ **6.** ice cream   **f.** carton or container
_____ **7.** milk   **g.** stick or tub
_____ **8.** butter   **h.** bottle

GRAMMAR CHECK

much/many—a little/a few

Use _much_ and _a little_ with noncount nouns.
   How **much** ice cream would you like? Just **a little**.

Use _many_ and _a few_ with count nouns.
   How **many** cookies would you like? Just **a few**.
For count nouns you can say _a couple_ (2), _a few_ (3–4) or _several_ (4–5). Or you can give an exact number: Let's buy _three_ tomatoes and _several_ carrots.

You can say _a lot_ for both count and noncount nouns:
   We need to buy **a lot of** cookies and **a lot of** cake.

⑤ Say It Practice the conversation with a partner.

A: How much <u>coffee</u> do you want?
B: Not much. Just a little.

A: How many <u>cookies</u> would you like?
B: Not many. Just a few.

Practice the conversation again. Use the pictures below.

    1   2   3

    4   5   6

6 Write Complete the sentences with *much, many, a little, a few,* or *a lot of.*
1. How _____ milk do you want in your coffee?
2. How _____ cookies do you want?
3. He doesn't have _____ money in his wallet.
4. She doesn't get _____ mail.
5. How _____ shirts does he have? He has _____ shirts.
6. I don't want _____ sugar. Just _____.
7. We are having a Thanksgiving dinner in _____ days.
8. I have to go. I don't have _____ time.

GRAMMAR CHECK

> ### some/any
>
> Use *some* for positive statements. Use *any* for questions and negative statements.
>
> **Question:** Is there **any** ice cream in the freezer?
> **Positive:** Yes, there is **some** ice cream in the freezer.
> **Negative:** No, there isn't **any** ice cream in the freezer.
>
> **Exceptions:** For requests or offers, always use *some*:
> Would you like **some** coffee? Can I have **some** sugar, please?

7 Write Complete the sentences with *some* or *any.*
1. Is there _____ stuffing on the table?
2. There is _____ corn in the bowl.
3. We don't have _____ milk in the refrigerator.
4. There are _____ mashed potatoes in the kitchen.
5. Can I have _____ corn, please?
6. Are there _____ cookies left?
7. Would you like _____ cookies?
8. There isn't _____ turkey on his plate.

8 Teamwork Task Work in teams of four. Fill out the chart below for one student volunteer (Student 1).
Student 2: Ask about noncount nouns. (Is there any milk in your kitchen?)
Student 3: Ask about count nouns. (Are there any apples in your kitchen?)
Student 4: Ask how much or how many. (How much milk is in your refrigerator?)

STUDENT 1	WHAT'S IN THE KITCHEN?	HOW MUCH OR HOW MANY?

Homework

Make a list of things in your kitchen. Use *there is/are* and *a, an,* or *some.*

What Do We Need from the Market?

Lesson 2

1 **Say It** Practice the conversation with a partner.

A: What do we need from the market?

B: Why don't you buy <u>some grapes</u> and <u>a watermelon</u>?

A: OK. Do we need any <u>bananas</u>?

B: No, we already have <u>some bananas</u>.

Practice the conversation again. Use the pictures below.

1

2

3

> **Note:** *a/an or some*
> Use *some* for noncount nouns in affirmative statements.
> Use *some* for plural count nouns in affirmative statements.
> Use *a/an* for singular count nouns.

2 **Write** Complete the sentences with *a, an,* or *some.*

1. We need _____ bread.
2. She wants to buy _____ apple.
3. I'm going to cook _____ spaghetti.
4. We need to buy _____ mushrooms and _____ onion.
5. He's going to buy _____ oranges and _____ beans.
6. They're going to cook _____ eggplant.

3 **Listen** Listen to the conversations and check your answers to Activity 2.

4 **Listen** Listen and circle the beverages you hear. Then tell the class what Jessica's family likes to drink.

5 **Say It** Practice the conversation with a partner.

for breakfast?

A: What do you like to drink <u>for breakfast</u>?

B: I like to drink <u>coffee</u>. How about you?

A: I like to drink <u>tea</u>.

B: What do you like to eat <u>for breakfast</u>?

A: I like to eat <u>pancakes</u>. How about you?

B: I like to eat <u>ham and eggs in the morning</u>.

Practice the conversation again. Use the pictures below.

1. **for dinner?**   2. **on hot days?**

6 **Group Practice** Work in groups of five or six. Ask people in your group what they like to drink – in the morning, in the afternoon, in the evening, late at night, on hot days, on cold days, and at parties or celebrations.

Tell the class what beverages your group drinks the most.

Infinitives

To + the base form of a verb = the infinitive
to go, to eat, to drink, to buy, to cook

Some verbs can be followed by an infinitive. Some common verbs that take infinitives are *want, need, like, love, hate, would like, have.*

I *need* **to buy** some groceries.   He *hates* **to eat** spinach.

7 **Write** Complete the sentences below with an infinitive and a noun.

1. I like <u>to eat pizza</u>   .
2. I want _____ .
3. I need _____ .
4. I hate _____ .
5. I would like _____ .

8 **Pair Practice** Work with a partner. Put the words in correct order to make a question. Then ask your partner the questions.

1. eat for What want to lunch do you

   _____?

2. the need supermarket do we from What to buy

   _____?

3. weekends What hate to on you do do

   _____?

4. What class do after have you do to

   _____?

9 **Group Practice** *Find someone who . . .* Work in a large group or with the whole class. Ask other students questions to complete the sentences below. Write their names.

Example: *Ana:* Do you like to drink coffee in the morning?
             Paul: Yes, I do.
             Liza: No, I don't.

1. <u>Paul</u>_____ likes to drink coffee in the morning.
2. _____ wants to go shopping for groceries this weekend.
3. _____ loves to eat ice cream.
4. _____ doesn't like to drink milk.
5. _____ has to cook dinner tonight.
6. _____ likes to drink orange juice every morning.
7. _____ would like to eat in a restaurant tonight.

be going to: questions and short answers

Is	he / she / it	**going to**	cook	chicken?	Yes, he is. / No, he isn't.
Are	we / you / they	**going to**	eat	fish?	Yes, we are. / No, we aren't.
Am	I		**going to**	buy	groceries?	Yes, you are. / No, you aren't.

Check Points:
✓ Use *be going + infinitive* to talk about future plans.
✓ When the main verb is *go,* you can drop the infinitive from the sentence.
  I'm **going to go** to the market. = I'm **going** to the market.

10 Say It Practice the conversation with a partner.

A: Where are you going?

B: I'm going to <u>the Downtown Market</u>.

A: What are you going to buy?

B: I'm going to buy <u>some Maximum Coffee</u>. <u>It's 30%</u> off.

A: How much <u>is it</u>?

B: The regular price is <u>$9.00</u>, but today <u>it's</u> only <u>$6.30</u>.

A: That's a great price.

Practice the conversation again. Use the pictures below.

1

2

11 Write Answer the questions. Write complete sentences.

1. When are you going to the market? _____ .

2. What vegetables are you going to buy? _____ .

3. What beverages are you going to buy? _____ .

4. What else are you going to buy? _____ .

5. How much are you going to spend? _____ .

6. What are you going to eat tomorrow? _____ .

7. What are you going to drink tomorrow? _____ .

Note: The U.S. government says that food products need to list the **ingredients** in order of quantity. The ingredient with the largest amount is listed first.

Cholesterol is a kind of fat that is in some foods. Fried foods, butter, cookies, and ice cream are high in cholesterol. Lean meat and most fruits and vegetables are low in cholesterol. Low cholesterol is desirable in most people's diets.

12 **Write** Answer the questions about the soup.

1. Which ingredient is found in the largest amount? _____

2. Does the soup have more salt or celery? _____

3. Which ingredient is found in the smallest amount? _____

4. Is there more cooked chicken or rice? _____

5. How much fat does the soup have? _____

6. How much protein does it have? _____

7. Would you like to taste this soup? Why or why not?

_____

13 **Teamwork Task** Work in teams of three or four. Pretend you are going to make a delicious "Teacher Soup" for your class. First, decide what kind of soup you are going to make. Then make a list of the ingredients in your soup. Include vegetables and other things you like. Then fill out the shopping list below for things you are going to buy to make your "Teacher Soup."

Ingredients	How much/How many?
_____	_____
_____	_____
_____	_____
_____	_____
_____	_____

Game Time

Practice your grammar for count and noncount nouns. Pretend you are going to the supermarket after class. Tell the class what you are going to buy. Use *a* or *an* for count nouns and *some* for noncount nouns. Say as many things as you can in one minute. If you make a grammar mistake, stop!

What Would You Like?

Note: A *tip* is money you give the waiter or waitress for serving you. A tip is generally 15–20% of the check, before taxes.

1 Read Read this e-mail from Jessica's friend Lisa.

Hi Jessica!

Thank you for your e-mail. It was nice to hear from you. I'm glad you like your new job. My job is pretty good, too. I am a waitress in a very nice steak and seafood restaurant. Do you like seafood? The food in the restaurant is delicious.

My job is part-time. I work only 4 1/2 hours a day, but the pay is good because I get a lot of tips. I usually make about $20 an hour in tips. I work in the evening so I can go to school during the day. The job is pretty easy, but it doesn't have any health-care benefits. But the food is good. I get to eat dinner at the restaurant for free. Maybe that is a benefit!

I live in Austin, Texas, now. It's a very nice city. It's sunny and warm, and the people are very friendly. Why don't you come down and visit me sometime?

Your pal,
Lisa

T E X A S

☆
Austin

2 Write Answer the questions about the e-mail with complete sentences.

1. What does Lisa do? _____ .

2. Where does she work? _____ .

3. Where does she live? _____ .

4. How many hours does she work? _____ .

5. What does she like about her job? _____ .

6. Would you like her job? Why or why not? _____

_____

Like vs. would like

Like expresses an opinion:
   I **like** pizza. He/She **likes** pizza.

Would like expresses a want or desire:
   Would you **like** pizza tonight?
   Yes, I **would like** pizza.
   He/She **would like** pizza.

③ Pair Practice Work with a partner. Ask and answer questions about foods your partner likes and foods your partner would like now.

Example: *Student 1:* Do you like chocolate ice cream?
   Student 2: Yes, I do. (*or* No, I don't.)
   Student 1: Would you like some chocolate ice cream now?
   Student 2: Yes, I would. (*or* No, I wouldn't.)

Ask about:

1. pizza
2. apple juice
3. onions
4. strawberries
5. rice and beans
6. lettuce
7. milk
8. mashed potatoes
9. a turkey sandwich

④ Write Complete the sentences with *would, do, like/likes,* or *would like.*

1. _____ you like some more coffee now? Yes, please.

2. _____ you like coffee after dinner? Yes, I _____.

3. _____ you like donuts for breakfast? No, I _____.

4. _____ you like to cook outside in the summer? Yes, I love to.

5. We _____ some more bread, please. Certainly.

6. What vegetables does she _____? Well, she _____ corn very much.

⑤ Group Practice Work in groups of four or five. Ask your classmates what restaurants they like. Ask how often they go to those restaurants and what they like to eat or drink there. Ask what restaurant they would like to go to next weekend.

Tell the class about one of your classmates' favorite restaurant.

6 Pair Practice Work with a partner. Ask your partner what foods and beverages he likes from the Downtown International Restaurant menu. Ask which ones he/she doesn't like.

Appetizers

Vietnamese Shrimp Rolls	$5.00
Calamari	$5.00
Sushi	$6.00
Pork Ribs	$4.00

DOWNTOWN INTERNATIONAL RESTAURANT

Entrees

Kung Pao Chicken	$9.00
Shrimp Tempura	$8.00
Lasagna	$8.00
Beef Kabob	$8.50
Falafel	$8.00
Chicken Enchilada	$6.00

Beverages

Soda	$2.00	Black Tea	$1.00
Juice	$1.50	Green Tea	$1.00
Cappuccino	$3.00	Espresso	$2.00

Soups

Clam Chowder	$3.00
Lobster Bisque	$4.00
Minestrone	$3.00
Won Ton	$3.50
French Onion	$4.00

Desserts

Cheesecake	$5.00
Baklava	$4.00
Chocolate Pudding	$4.00
Tiramisu	$4.00
Almond Cookie	$4.00
Ice Cream	$3.00

7 Listen Listen to the conversations from the Downtown International Restaurant. Pretend you are the waiter or waitress. Write down the orders you hear on the check below. Include the price. Add up the check.

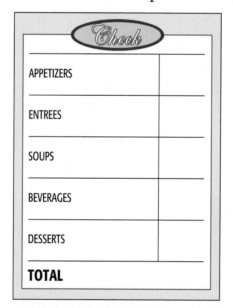

Check

APPETIZERS	
ENTREES	
SOUPS	
BEVERAGES	
DESSERTS	
TOTAL	

GRAMMAR CHECK

Infinitive or gerund?

Like can be followed by an infinitive or a gerund (verb + *-ing* used as a noun).

Like + infinitive: I like **to cook**.

Like + gerund: I like **cooking**.

Would like can be followed by an infinitive but **not** by a gerund.

I would like **to cook** dinner. (Correct)

I would like **cooking** dinner. (*Not* correct)

8 **Write** Fix the mistakes in the incorrect sentences. If the sentence is correct, write *correct*.

1. I like pizza very much.

_____

2. I would like buying a pizza.

_____

3. She likes cooking very much.

_____

4. She would like cook dinner for you.

_____

5. I would like having some coffee, please.

_____

6. She like to buy a chocolate ice cream.

_____

7. He would likes to order dinner.

_____

8. I like eat dinner in a restaurant.

_____

9 **Teamwork Task** Work in teams of four. Pretend you are a waiter or waitress at the Downtown International Restaurant. The other teammates look at the menu on page 55. Ask them what they would like to drink. Ask if they are ready to order. Ask about appetizers. Ask what they would like for dinner. Ask about dessert.

Write your teammates' orders on the check below. Include prices. Add up the check. How much did they spend?

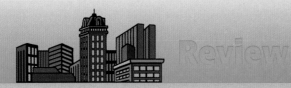

1 Read and Listen Read the story. Then listen to the story.

Delicious!

Jessica misses some of the food she used to eat in Colombia. She misses her mother's coconut rice the most. But she likes the supermarkets and restaurants in her new neighborhood very much. When she has time, she likes to walk slowly around a supermarket and look at all the different kinds of delicious food they have. And she loves to taste new things. Last night she tried an avocado, a Thai chicken salad, and some grilled swordfish for the first time, and they were all delicious.

Jessica really likes eating at new restaurants. But tonight she isn't going to a restaurant. She is going to stay home and cook. She is going to surprise her family by making her special Colombian soup. She is going to include some pieces of chicken and a few carrots. She is going to add a couple of potatoes, a tomato, and some mushrooms. And then she's going to put in a little salt and some special Colombian spices. It is going to be delicious!

2 Write Write complete answers to the questions below.

1. What food does Jessica miss from Colombia the most?

   _____ .

2. What does she like to do in supermarkets? _____ .

3. Does Jessica like grilled swordfish? _____ .

4. Where does Jessica like to eat? _____ .

5. Where is she going to eat tonight? _____ .

6. How much chicken is she going to put in? _____ .

7. How many potatoes is she going to add? _____ .

CRITICAL THINKING:

8. Would you like to taste Jessica's Colombian soup? Why or why not?

   _____ .

3 Write Write an e-mail to Jessica. Tell her what foods you like and don't like. Tell her if there is any food you miss from your country. Tell her about some special food from your country. Tell her how to make it. What ingredients should she put in?

4 Best Answer Bubble the correct answer.

a b c

1. There isn't _____ coffee in the cabinet.
   a) many   **b)** some   **c)** any   ○ ○ ○

2. There are _____ cookies.
   a) a   **b)** some   **c)** a lot   ○ ○ ○

3. There aren't _____ apples on the table.
   a) much   **b)** some   **c)** many   ○ ○ ○

4. What do we need _____ at the market?
   a) buy   **b)** buying   **c)** to buy   ○ ○ ○

5. What would you like _____?
   a) eat   **b)** eating   **c)** to eat   ○ ○ ○

5 Write Write the correct words for the objects in the picture.

1. _____	6. _____
2. _____	7. _____
3. _____	8. _____
4. _____	9. _____
5. _____	10. _____

6 Write Work with a partner to complete the dialogue.

A: I'm going to the Downtown Market.

B: What _____ to buy?

A: Whatever we need. What _____ you like me to get?

B: I'd like a _____ and a _____, and some _____ and _____, too.

A: OK. Anything else? Do we have _____ bread?

B: No, we need _____ bread. And I'd also like _____ and _____.

A: OK. Just make a list and I'll get everything.

7 Pair Practice Practice the conversation in Activity 6 with a partner.

8 Teamwork Task Work in teams of three or four. Pretend your team is going to have a party for your teacher's birthday. Discuss what you need to buy for the party. Will you bring special food from your own culture? Make a shopping list of food, drinks, and desserts you are going to buy. Include how much or how many of each thing you are going to buy.

FOOD	DRINKS	DESSERTS
_____	_____	_____
_____	_____	_____
_____	_____	_____
_____	_____	_____
_____	_____	_____
_____	_____	_____

🎧 **Pronunciation** Reduction: *Gonna* instead of *going to*

Many native speakers join words together when they speak. They make two words sound like one word. Native speakers often say *gonna* instead of *going to*.

A. Listen and repeat the following sentences.
   1. The family's going to have dinner.
   2. Jessica's going to set the table.
   3. She's going to make potatoes.
   4. They're going to have ice cream.

B. Work with a partner. Tell your partner some things you are going to do. Say *gonna* instead of *going to*.

INTERNET IDEA

Nutrition Information

Search the Internet for information on nutrition. Find out about good and bad cholesterol, protein, carbohydrates, and fruit and vegetables. Pick one of these areas of interest and report your findings to the class.

I can . . .			
• identify places in the kitchen.	1	2	3
• identify common Thanksgiving foods.	1	2	3
• identify common beverages.	1	2	3
• distinguish between count and noncount nouns.	1	2	3
• interpret food labels.	1	2	3
• give and take restaurant orders.	1	2	3
• read ads and coupons.	1	2	3
• write a shopping list.	1	2	3
• work together to plan a party.	1	2	3

1 = not well   2 = OK   3 = very well

DOWNTOWN

9 **Write** Write the missing words in the cartoon story. Use these words: *some, much, many, food, like* (2), *Would, to cook, to have, going to, is.*

Cindy: Next week is Alberto's birthday. I want (1) _____ a nice party for him.
Rosa: Great. Who are you (2) _____ invite?

Cindy: Everybody!
Rosa: Everybody? How (3) _____ people is that?
Cindy: I don't know. I'd (4) _____ to have a really big party.

Rosa: So, what kind of (5) _____ are you going to have at this big party? Some salad? A cake?
Cindy: Well, first I'm going to buy (6) _____ chocolate ice cream. Alberto loves chocolate ice cream.

Rosa: How (7)_____ ice cream?
Cindy: At least four or five gallons.
Rosa: This kind of ice cream is expensive.
Cindy. Look at the price!

Cindy: Maybe you're right. Maybe I don't need five gallons!
Rosa: And what are you going (8) _____for all those people? Cooking for a lot of people is a lot of work!

Cindy: Maybe I'll buy one gallon of ice cream and have a party for two.
Rosa: (9) _____ you like to make it four? David and I (10) _____ ice cream!
Cindy: Maybe four really good friends (11) _____ enough!

10 **Pair Practice** Practice the story with a partner.

Housing

GOALS

- ✓ Identify and describe furniture
- ✓ Talk about housing needs and wants
- ✓ Read and interpret rental ads
- ✓ Compare homes using comparative adjectives
- ✓ Use *there was / there were*
- ✓ Call to ask about a rental ad
- ✓ Complain about a housing problem
- ✓ Read and interpret a lease
- ✓ Negotiate a lease agreement
- ✓ Write a rental ad

1 Read *Read the story. Match the numbers in the picture to the words in the box.*

Home

Jessica lives in a three-bedroom house with her aunt, uncle, and two cousins. The house has a family room that Jessica uses as her bedroom. There is a dresser and a window with mini blinds in her room, but there isn't a closet because it isn't really a bedroom—it's a family room. A family room is an extra room, usually used as an informal living room or a playroom for children. Jessica's room also has a night table and a desk. And of course there is a bed with a bedspread and two fluffy pillows. The living room is more modern than Jessica's living room in Colombia. There is a fireplace with a lot of family photos on the mantle. And the living room has a skylight! Sometimes she sits in the living room and looks up at the stars through the skylight. The yard isn't as big as Jessica's yard in Colombia and the garden isn't as pretty. But the yard has a grill, and Jessica likes to have barbecues with her "American" family.

Listen 🎧

_____ yard
_____ fireplace
_____ garden
_____ grill
_____ mantle
_____ garage
_____ wall unit
_____ bedspread
_____ sofa
_____ dresser
_____ night table
_____ alarm clock
_____ floor lamp
_____ skylight
_____ photos
_____ desk
_____ end table
_____ coffee table
_____ pillows
_____ mini blinds

Is There a Swimming Pool?

FOR RENT

3-bedroom house with 2 baths and a family room. Modern kitchen, 2-car garage, yard with garden.

Price: $$$$

Jessica's home in Los Angeles

FOR RENT

2-bedroom apartment, 5th floor. Nice view. 1 bath. Large but old kitchen, Pool. Parking for 1 car

Price: $$

Jessica's home in Colombia

1 **Say It** Practice the conversation with a partner.

A: Is there <u>a swimming pool</u> at Jessica's new home?

B: No, there isn't.

A: Was there <u>a swimming pool</u> at Jessica's old home?

B: Yes, there was.

A: Is there <u>a swimming pool</u> at your home?

B: _____

Practice the conversation again. Use the photographs below.

1

2

3

GRAMMAR CHECK

there is/was and there are/were

	Singular	Plural
Present tense	**there is**	**there are**
Past tense	**there was**	**there were**

Present tense: **There are** many *trees* at my new house. **There is** a *garage,* too. **Is there** a family *room?*

Past tense: **There were** two English *teachers* at my old school. **Was there** a French *teacher?* No, but **there was** one Spanish *teacher.*

2 **Write** Change the sentences from present to past.

1. There is a sofa in Jessica's living room. _____.

2. Are there two bathrooms in your home? _____?

3. Is there a lamp in your bedroom? _____?

4. There are some flowers in Jessica's garden. _____.

5. Are there any windows in your bedroom? _____?

6. There is a table in my dining room. _____.

3 **Group Practice** Work in groups of four or five. Ask other students questions about their homes now and their homes in their countries. Ask as many questions as you can.

Example: *Student 1:* Is there a desk in your bedroom now?

Student 2: Yes, there is.

Student 1: Was there a desk in your home in (Mexico)?

Student 2: No, there wasn't.

4 **Write** Write these adjectives under the correct pictures: *antique, modern, beautiful, ugly, expensive, cheap, fancy,* and *plain*. Then write a sentence about each item using the adjective and noun.

antique _____   _____   _____   _____

_____   _____   _____   _____

1. <u>There was an antique rocking chair in my grandmother's house</u> .

2. _____.

3. _____.

4. _____.

5. _____.

6. _____.

7. _____.

8. _____.

Note: Adjective Word Order

In English, adjectives usually come before the nouns they describe:
a *comfortable* chair, a *big* house, a *pretty green* flower

Exception: When the noun and adjective are separated by the verb *to be*, the adjective comes after the verb: The flowers *are* **beautiful**. That house *was* **big!**

5 **Write** Write the sentences in the correct word order.

1. There kitchen modern in is a house Jessica's.

   _____

2. two were desks cheap There in his bedroom.

   _____

3. man tall garden beautiful has The a.

   _____

4. Her beautiful is furniture living room.

   _____

5. was dresser very expensive The.

   _____

6 **Pair Practice** Work with a partner. Take turns describing things in your classroom. Use an adjective and a noun.

Example: *Student 1:* There's a large chalkboard in our classroom.
   Student 2: Yes, and there are five old tables.

7 **Write** Look at the descriptions of Jessica's two homes on page 64. Answer the questions about Jessica's two homes.

1. Which one is bigger?   Jessica's Los Angeles home is bigger   .
2. Which kitchen is more modern?   _____.
3. Which one is cheaper?   _____.
4. Which one is more expensive?   _____.
5. Which one has a nicer view?   _____.
6. Which one do you like better?   _____.

Culture Tip

Rent or buy?

Sixty-eight percent of American households own their homes. A home may be a single-family home, a two-family home, or a condo. The rest of the population rents their home or apartment. Do you rent or own your own home?

Comparative adjectives

Adjective	Comparative Form	Examples
one-syllable	add -er	**smaller, higher, greener**
two-syllable ending in -y	drop -y, add -ier	**prettier, tinier**
other two-or-more-syllable adjectives	use **more** + adjective OR **less** + adjective	**more interesting** **more unusual** **less comfortable** **less confusing**
Irregular: **good, bad, far**	irregular	**better, worse, farther**

8 **Listen** Listen to the following words. How many syllables do you hear? Write the words in the correct column below.

ONE SYLLABLE	TWO SYLLABLES ENDING IN -Y	TWO OR MORE SYLLABLES
_____	_____	_____
_____	_____	_____
_____	_____	_____
_____	_____	_____

9 **Write** Write the comparative form of the adjectives in parentheses.

1. My sofa is _____ than Lin's sofa. (new)
2. His garden is _____ than her garden. (beautiful)
3. Lin's living room is _____ than Jessica's living room. (dark)
4. My bedroom is _____ than Alex's bedroom. (sunny)
5. My sofa is _____ than my arm chair. (comfortable)
6. Jessica's yard is _____ than my yard. (interesting)
7. The location of my home is _____ than his location. (good)
8. Her neighborhood is _____ than his. (safe)
9. The streets are _____ near his house. (busy)
10. Her view is a lot _____ than his. (bad)

10 **Teamwork Task** Work in teams of four or five. Choose two student volunteers. Ask the volunteers questions about their homes and fill out the chart. Then work together to write comparative sentences about the two homes. Write as many sentences as you can.

	Student 1's Home	Student 2's Home
Size (How many rooms?)	_____	_____
Location (How far from school?)	_____	_____
Kitchen (Modern or old?)	_____	_____
Living room (Bright or dark?)	_____	_____
Bedroom (Big or small?)	_____	_____

How Do You Like Your Apartment?

1 Say It Practice the conversation with a partner.

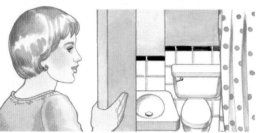

small / large

A: How do you like your apartment?

B: The <u>bathroom</u> is too <u>small</u>. I'd like an apartment with a <u>larger bathroom</u>.

A: Well, I'm sure you can find one.

B: I hope so!

Practice the conversation again. Use the pictures below.

1. old-fashioned / modern   2. dark / bright   3. ugly / pretty

2 Write Read about the problems Tania has with her apartment. Use an opposite comparative adjective to tell what she wants to have.

1. Her kitchen appliances are too old.

   She would like newer kitchen appliances .

2. Her neighborhood is too dangerous.

   _____ .

3. Her rent is too expensive.

   _____ .

4. Her neighbors are too noisy.

   _____ .

5. Her wallpaper is too ugly.

   _____ .

> **Note:** ***Too*** and ***very***
> *Too* means excessive. *Too* shows there is a problem:
> The weather is **too** hot. I don't like it.
> *Very* means a lot or a large amount of something.
> He's **very** strong. He exercises every day.

3 **Write** Complete the sentences with *too* or *very*.

1. The weather in my city is _____ hot. But I love hot weather.

2. That TV is _____ expensive. I can't afford it.

3. My bed is _____ old. It's a valuable antique.

4. My dishwasher is _____ old. It doesn't work anymore.

5. My kitchen appliances aren't old. They work _____ well.

6. My son is _____ young to get a driver's license. He's 14.

7. The carpet is _____ soft. It feels nice under my feet.

4 **Say It** Practice the conversation with a partner.

A: This <u>TV</u> is <u>bigger</u> than that <u>TV</u>.

B: You're right. That one isn't <u>as big as</u> this one.

A: This <u>TV</u> is also <u>more expensive</u>.

B: You're right. That one isn't <u>as expensive as</u> this one.

big / expensive

Practice the conversation again. Use the pictures below.

1. **new / efficient**   2. **tall / bright**

GRAMMAR CHECK

As . . . as comparisons	
Use *as . . . as* comparisons to show that two things are equal.	Your kitchen is **as big as** my kitchen. Her kitchen is **as big as** my garage.
Use *as . . . as* comparisons with a negative verb to show that two things are less than equal.	Your kitchen isn't **as big as** my kitchen. = My kitchen is bigger.

5 **Write** Change the positive comparatives to negative *as . . . as* comparisons.

1. My kitchen is larger than my bathroom.

   <u>My bathroom isn't as large as my kitchen</u>   .

2. The town's garden is more beautiful than my garden.

   _____ .

3. José's apartment is closer to school than Tina's apartment.

   _____ .

4. His kitchen is more modern than his bathroom.

   _____ .

5. Jessica's neighborhood is quieter than Alex's neighborhood.

   _____ .

6 **Listen** Mara lives in Manhattan and is thinking about moving to Brooklyn. She is thinking about her apartment in Manhattan and an apartment in Brooklyn. She needs to decide which one is better. Listen to the conversation. Fill in the missing information about the two apartments below.

	Manhattan	Brooklyn
Building	old	_____
Floor	_____	8th floor
Cost	_____	_____
Air-conditioning	no	_____
Laundry room	_____	_____
Safety	a little dangerous	_____
Location	not far from work	_____

7 **Write** Use the information in Activity 6 to write ten comparisons between the two apartments. Write five positive comparisons and five negative comparisons (using *as . . . as*).

Positive

_____

_____

_____

_____

_____

Negative

_____

_____

_____

_____

_____

8 **Group Practice** Work in groups of four or six. Ask and answer questions about the city you live in now and the city you are from. First, ask students where they are from. Write their names and the names of their cities below. Then ask *which* questions about the two places.

Example: *Student 1:* Where do you live now and where are you from?
Student 2: I live in Miami and I am from San Juan, Puerto Rico.
Student 1: Which place is larger— Miami or San Juan?
Student 2: Miami is larger than San Juan **OR** San Juan isn't as large as Miami.

Practice questions and answers with all of your group members. Use this list of adjectives and nouns or use different adjectives: *clean, safe, dangerous, beautiful, ugly, cheap, expensive, interesting, boring, friendly, noisy, quiet, tall buildings,* and *good restaurants*

Name	Native City	Current City

Game Time

Three Adjectives
One student thinks of a place and writes three adjectives about it on the board or a piece of paper. The other students in the group try to guess the place. Take turns until everyone in the group has had a chance to think of a place.

Call the Manager

1 **Read** Read the e-mail from Freddy, Jessica's classmate.

Hello Jessica,

Thanks for writing to me about your job. It sounds very good—a lot more interesting than mine. I am working as an apartment manager in a building with forty-five apartments. The first part of my job is to show and rent the apartments. Second, I collect the rent. And third, I fix small problems in people's apartments like dripping faucets and broken locks. For bigger, more difficult repair problems I call a professional repair person.

Sometimes it's easy to rent the empty apartments, but sometimes it can be difficult. Some tenants think the kitchen appliances are too old. Some people think the bedrooms aren't bright enough. Some people think the swimming pool isn't big enough, or the building isn't as modern as they would like, or the rent isn't as cheap as they would like.

I'm sure that my pay isn't as high as yours, but I do get a free apartment to live in, so I guess the benefits are pretty good.

See you in class on Monday!

Your friend,

Freddy

2 **Write** Answer the questions with complete sentences.

1. What is Freddy's job title?

_____

2. What are Freddy's job duties?

_____

3. What kind of problems does Freddy fix?

_____

4. What kind of kitchen appliances do some tenants want?

_____

5. What kind of bedrooms do some tenants want?

_____

6. What kind of swimming pool would some tenants like?

_____

CRITICAL THINKING:
7. Would you like to live in Freddy's building? Why or why not?

_____

> **Note: Too** and **enough**
> *Too* and *enough* are usually used with adjectives that are opposites:
> The apartment is **too small**. It isn't **big enough.**
> Is he **old enough** to drive? No, he's **too young**.

③ Read Read about the apartment Jessica wants. Then read the rental ads below.

What I'm looking for is a one-bedroom apartment for under $1,000 in a quiet neighborhood, close to my job downtown or close to the beach. I want a large, modern kitchen with new appliances. I'd also like to live in a fairly new building with a garage and a security gate. I'd really like to live on the 5th or 6th floor in an apartment with a nice view.

<table>
<tr><td align="center">

Apartment for ★ Rent/Lease ★

5640 Colorado Blvd. First Floor
1 bdrm, 1 bath, Small kitchen
Close to mountains,
45 min. from downtown
Available immediately
Call: 818-555-3456 **$1,150/mo.**

</td><td align="center">

Apartment for ★ Rent: April 1 ★

955 Sunset Blvd.
Second Floor Studio apt.
Nice old building near downtown
Antique kitchen/bath
Beautiful yard with garden
$995/mo.

</td></tr>
</table>

④ Teamwork Task Work in teams of four. Decide what's wrong with these apartments for Jessica. Two team members write as many things as they can about the first apartment, and the other two write about the second one. Write complete sentences with "too" or "enough." Then discuss and decide together which apartment is better for Jessica. Report to the class.

Colorado Boulevard

_____

_____

_____

_____

_____

Sunset Boulevard

_____

_____

_____

_____

_____

5 Say It Practice the conversation with a partner.

A: Can I help you?

B: Yes, I'm looking for a one-bedroom apartment near the beach. Do you have one?

A: Well, I have a nice two-bedroom apartment near the beach.

B: I think that's probably too big for me.

A: It has a beautiful modern kitchen and bathroom. And it has a two-car garage and a laundry room.

B: How much is the rent?

A: The rent is $1,200 a month. Would you like to see it?

B: No, that's too expensive. Do you have something cheaper?

A: Well, I also have . . .

> **2 Bedroom Apt. near beach**
> Beautiful modern kitchen, bath
> 2-car garage
> laundry rm.
> **$1200 Mo.**

6 Listen Listen to the conversations. Fill in the missing information in the rental ads below.

FOR RENT
Studio apt. _____
_____ stove
and _____ .
Large _____ with
_____ garden.
$850

1

FOR RENT
_____ bedroom, 2 _____
in Hollywood. _____ floor,
new bldg. Very nice _____ .
Large _____
and bath. Pool.
$1,000

2

FOR RENT
3 bdrm. _____
in great _____ .
2 _____ baths.
Balcony, _____
Must see.
$1,300

3

7 Pair Practice Work with a partner. Ask and answer questions about the rental ads above.

Word Help: Apartment problems

leaky faucet — broken window — clogged toilet — broken lock — broken heater — mice, ants

8 Match Match the problems with the results.

_____ 1. a leaky faucet   **a.** I can't lock the door.

_____ 2. a clogged toilet   **b.** I can't turn it on.

_____ 3. a broken window   **c.** I can't turn it off.

_____ 4. a broken lock   **d.** I can't flush it.

_____ 5. a broken heater   **e.** I can't get rid of them.

_____ 6. mice and ants   **f.** I can't close it.

9 Say It Practice the conversation with a partner.

A: Hello. This is Lin in Apartment 2C.

B: What can I do for you, Lin?

A: I have <u>a leaky faucet. I can't turn it off</u>.

B: OK. I'll take a look at it tomorrow.

A: Can you come sooner than that? It's really a problem.

B: OK. I'll try to be there about 7:00 tonight.

Practice more conversations. Use the pictures in the Word Help on page 74.

> **Note:** A lease is a contract to use a building for a period of time

10 Read Read the lease agreement on page 76. Then answer the questions.

1. Who is going to rent this apartment? _____

2. When does the lease begin? _____

3. How long is the lease? _____

4. How much does the tenant have to pay each month? _____

5. When should the tenant pay her rent? _____

6. Who pays for the water in this apartment?_____

7. When should the owner return the security deposit? _____

8. Can the tenant have a cat in this apartment? _____

9. What time should tenant stop playing loud music? _____

10. What time should people leave the pool area? _____

11. Who pays for the utilities in this apartment? _____

CRITICAL THINKING:

12. Do you think the lease is fair or unfair? _____

13. What other apartment rules can you add to the lease?_____

_____

Lease

This is a contract made between the building owner <u>George W. Ross</u> and tenant <u>Tania Petrova</u>.

Tenant agrees to rent from owner a <u>two-bedroom</u>, <u>one-bath apartment</u> in the city of <u>Santa Monica</u>, state of <u>California</u>, at <u>1525 Montana Avenue, Unit 3A</u>, in excellent condition.

Term: The term will begin on April 10, 2006, and continue for one year until April 10, 2007.

Rent: Rent will be $1,050 per month, payable on the tenth of each month.

Utilities: Tenant will pay for utilities (= gas and electricity). Owner will pay for water.

Pets: Tenant may not have pets in the apartment, except with permission from owner.

Sublet: Tenant may not sublet (= rent or lease to someone else) the apartment without written permission from owner.

Security Deposit: Tenant will give a security deposit equal to one month's rent ($1,050) to owner before the first day of occupancy. Deposit will be returned to tenant on last day of occupancy, after inspection of property.

Other Rules: Tenants may use pool between 7 A.M. and 11 P.M. Children under ten years may not be left in pool area without a parent or guardian present. Tenant may not play loud music, television, or other electronic equipment before 8 A.M. or after 10 P.M. Owner may enter and inspect apartment with one-day written notice.

Owner: *George W. Ross*   Date: *April 5, 2006*

Tenant: *Tania Petrova*   Date: *April 5, 2007*

 Read and Listen Read the dialogue. Then listen to the dialogue.

Moving to a New Apartment

Tania: Hi, Jessica. I came over to tell you that I'm moving to a new apartment.

Jessica: You're moving? Why?

Tania: Many reasons. First of all, my apartment needs a lot of repairs, and my landlord isn't very good about making them. Also, the bedroom is too dark. The kitchen is very, very old. And the bathroom isn't big enough. My new apartment is better; it has a nicer and prettier living room and a great view of the neighborhood. It has three big windows, and my old apartment only has one!

Jessica: What about the neighborhood? Is it as nice as this one?

Tania: Well, this neighborhood is more interesting, I think. The people are younger and friendlier, but the neighborhood is further away from the beach. The new neighborhood is cleaner and safer, and is closer to the beach. You know how much I love the beach.

Jessica: What about the rent? Is it more expensive?

Tania: Well, yes. It's $200 more a month. The utility bills will be higher, too. But it's going to be closer to my work, so, I won't be late as much.

Jessica: That sounds great. When can I visit you?

Write Read the sentences. Circle True or False.

1. Tania's old apartment needs a lot of repairs.	True	False
2. Tania wants a more modern kitchen.	True	False
3. Tania's old apartment has a prettier living room.	True	False
4. Tania's new apartment has a brighter living room.	True	False
5. Tania's new neighborhood isn't as interesting as her old neighborhood.	True	False
6. Tania's new neighborhood is closer to the beach.	True	False
7. Tania's new neighborhood is cheaper.	True	False
8. Tania thinks the new apartment will be better.	True	False

CRITICAL THINKING:

9. Is it true or false that "You get what you pay for"? Why?	True	False

3 **Write** Compare the home and neighborhood you live in now with a home and neighborhood you lived in before. Write as many sentences as you can.

_____

_____

_____

_____

_____

_____

4 **Best Answer** Bubble the correct answer.   **a**   **b**   **c**

1. Curtains are _____ than miniblinds.   ○   ○   ○
   a) pretty   **b)** more pretty   **c)** prettier

2. The streets are _____ in Hollywood than in   ○   ○   ○
   Santa Monica.
   a) busyer   **b)** busier   **c)** more busy

3. The bedroom isn't as light _____ the living room.   ○   ○   ○
   a) than   **b)** as   **c)** more

4. The kitchen is too dark. It isn't _____ enough.   ○   ○   ○
   a) bright   **b)** new   **c)** hot

5. A lease tells how much you have to pay for _____.   ○   ○   ○
   a) rent   **b)** utilities   **c)** pets

6. A tenant is the person who _____ an apartment or home. ○   ○   ○
   a) rents   **b)** manages   **c)** owns

5 **Pair Practice** Work together to complete the dialogue. Then practice the dialogue with your partner.

A: Beachside Apartments. Can I help you?

B: Yes, I'm looking for a _____. Do you have one?

A: Yes, I do. What else are you looking for in the apartment?

B: I would like _____ and _____ and

_____.

A: This apartment has _____ and _____ but

it doesn't have _____. Would you like to see it?

B: I'm not sure. How _____?

A: It's $1,300 a month.

B: Oh. Do you have anything cheaper?

6 **Teamwork Task** Work in teams of four. Pretend you are a family of four. Work together to write an ad for the dream house or apartment you would like to rent. Describe everything you want in your home: location, size, special features. Don't include the cost of the rent.

_____

_____

_____

_____

_____

_____

_____

_____

7 **Teamwork Task** Work with the same team as in Activity 6. This time, two students are the tenants and two students are the building owners. Create a lease for your dream home. Include any rules you can agree on.

Lease

This is a contract made between the building owner _____

_____ and tenant _____.

Tenant agrees to rent from owner a _____

in the city of _____, state of _____,

at _____, in excellent condition.

Term: The term will begin on _____ and continue for

_____ until _____.

Rent: Rent will be _____ per month, payable on the _____ of each month

Utilities: _____

_____

Pets: _____

_____

Sublet: _____

_____

Security Deposit: Tenant shall give a security deposit _____

_____ to owner before the first day of occupancy.

Deposit will be returned to tenant _____.

Other Rules: _____

_____

Owner: _____   **Date:** _____

Tenant: _____   **Date:** _____

Pronunciation Short /i/ sound and long /e/ sound

Listen to the vowel sounds in these words. Some words have the short /i/ as in the word *live*. Others have the long /e/ sound as in the word *leave*.

A. Listen and repeat.

his	sit	cheap	feet	chip	seat
eat	he's	it	lick	fit	leak

B. Now listen to these word pairs. If the words are the same, write *S*. If they are different, write *D*.

1. _____   6. _____

2. _____   7. _____

3. _____   8. _____

4. _____   9. _____

5. _____   10. _____

INTERNET IDEA

Go to the Web site for your local newspaper. Look at the housing and rental ads in the Real Estate section. Find a house or apartment that matches the description you created in the Teamwork Task. Did you find one that matches, or almost matches? Did you find another house or apartment you would like to see? Go to a newspaper Web site in another city. Compare the apartment rent prices. Is the rent in your town cheaper or more expensive? Discuss with your class.

I can...			
• identify and describe furniture.	1	2	3
• talk about housing needs and wants.	1	2	3
• read and interpret rental ads.	1	2	3
• compare homes using comparatives adjectives.	1	2	3
• use *there was / there were*.	1	2	3
• call to ask about a rental ad.	1	2	3
• complain about a housing problem.	1	2	3
• read and interpret a lease.	1	2	3
• negotiate a lease agreement.	1	2	3
• write a rental ad.	1	2	3

1 = not well   2 = OK   3 = very well

8 Write
Write the missing words in the cartoon story. Use these words: *better, bigger, brighter, prettier, newer, nicer, modern, too, enough, more.*

Cindy: When we get married, Alberto, we're going to need a (1)_____ apartment. This place really isn't big (2)_____.
Alberto: OK.

Cindy: I want an apartment with a (3)_____ living room. This one is (4)_____ dark. And a (5)_____ bathroom. This one is really ugly.

Cindy: Also, the kitchen isn't very modern. I want a place with a (6)_____ (7)_____ kitchen.
Alberto: OK.

Alberto: What else would you like, dear?
Cindy: Maybe a place with a swimming pool or a (8)_____ yard. And I think we should get some (9)_____ furniture.

Alberto: My furniture isn't so old.
Cindy: That's true. Your TV is great. But I think we can get some (10)_____ things. What do you want in a new apartment, Alberto?

Alberto: Nothing.
Cindy: Nothing?
Alberto: Contigo, pan y agua.
Cindy: What does that mean, Alberto?
Alberto: It means "with you I need only bread and water!"

9 Pair Practice
Practice the story with a partner.

The Past

✓ Talk about past events

✓ Compare today with yesterday

✓ Use verbs in the past tense

✓ Ask and answer past tense questions

✓ Create a team story

✓ Describe a sequence of past events

✓ Describe past job duties

✓ Interpret a time line

✓ Create a personal and professional time line

1 Read and Listen *Look at the pictures and read the story. Then listen to the story. Then write a past tense sentence about each picture on the lines below.*

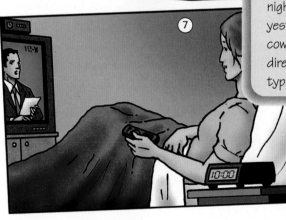

Yesterday

Yesterday was a typical weekday for Jessica. She usually gets up early during the week and yesterday she got up at 6:30. She always takes a shower before work, and she took one yesterday. She almost always drives to work and she drove yesterday, too. Most days she drinks a cup of coffee in the morning and she drank one yesterday. Most weekdays she works from 8:30 A.M. to 5:30 P.M. and she worked the same hours yesterday. On Monday nights she likes to cook dinner with her aunt and she cooked dinner with Lupe yesterday, too. At night she watches the news on TV at 10:00, and she watched it last night. But, there was something different about her day yesterday. On most weekdays Jessica eats lunch with her coworkers. But yesterday she ate lunch with the handsome director of an animation company. Maybe yesterday wasn't a typical weekday for Jessica after all!

What did Jessica do yesterday?

1. <u>Yesterday Jessica got up at 6:30</u>   .
2. _____ .
3. _____ .
4. _____ .
5. _____ .
6. _____ .
7. _____ .
8. _____ .

How Was Your Day?

Lesson 1

① Say It Practice the conversation with a partner.

washed the windows, cleaned out the garage

A: How was your day?

B: It was busy.

A: Why? What did you do?

B: I <u>washed the windows</u> and <u>cleaned out the garage</u> all day.

A: Is that all you did?

B: That was enough!

Practice the conversation again. Use the pictures below.

1. **worked, studied English**

2. **played music, watched TV**

GRAMMAR CHECK

Simple past tense—regular verbs

For most verbs, add **-ed** or **-d**: cook→cook**ed**, talk→talk**ed**, smile→smil**ed**.

For verbs that end in a consonant + **y**, change the **y** to **i** and add **-ed**: study→stud**ied**.

For most one-syllable verbs that end in a consonant-vowel-consonant, double the final consonant: stop→stop**ped**, drop→drop**ped**.

② Write Write the past tense of the verbs.

1. listen _____
2. rest _____
3. brush _____
4. dance _____
5. cry _____

6. shop _____
7. smile _____
8. try _____
9. talk _____
10. want _____

Pronunciation of regular past tense verbs

The endings of regular past tense verbs have three different pronunciations. Some endings sound like /t/: **walked**. Some sound like /d/: **played**. And some add a syllable and sound like /id/: **wanted**.

Check Point:
✓ Verbs whose present tense ends in a /t/ or /d/ sound add a syllable in the past tense. **Example:** rent–rent**ed** (pronounced "ren-tid")

3 Listen Listen and repeat the verbs. Practice the different ending sounds.

/t/	/d/	/id/
walked	played	wanted
worked	cleaned	needed
cooked	cried	rested
baked	called	painted

4 Listen Listen to the pronunciation of the following verbs. Write each verb in the correct column.

/t/	/d/	/id/
_____	_____	_____
_____	_____	_____
_____	_____	_____

5 Write Use verbs from Activities 3 and 4 to complete the sentences.

1. I _____ the dishes yesterday.
2. Lin _____ her teeth this morning.
3. David _____ to rock-and-roll music last night.
4. We _____ the kitchen blue last weekend.
5. Jessica _____ to her father three days ago.
6. Cindy _____ a delicious cake last night.
7. Manuel _____ roses last spring.

6 Pair Practice Work with a partner. Ask and answer questions about the people in Activity 5.

Example: *Student 1:* What did you wash yesterday?
   Student 2: I washed the dishes yesterday.

Make sure to use the correct ending pronunciation.

7 **Say It** Practice the conversation with a partner.

play, cook, rest

A: How was your weekend?

B: It was pretty good.

A: What did you do?

B: On Saturday I went to the park.

A: What did you do at the park?

B: First, <u>I played tennis</u>. Then I <u>cooked chicken on a barbecue grill</u>. And after that I <u>rested on my blanket</u> for a while.

A: You're right. It sounds like a pretty nice day.

Practice the conversations again. Use the pictures below.

1. watch, listen

Bill

2. talk, dance

8 **Listen** Listen to the sentences and write the verb you hear. Then circle if the time is yesterday or every day.

1. I _____ TV.	every day	yesterday
2. I _____ with my brother.	every day	yesterday
3. I _____ my teeth.	every day	yesterday
4. I _____ my uncle.	every day	yesterday
5. I _____ the dishes.	every day	yesterday
6. I _____ basketball.	every day	yesterday
7. I _____ a two-bedroom apartment.	every day	yesterday
8. I _____ to go to a party.	every day	yesterday

Word Help: Past time expressions

LAST	AGO	YESTERDAY
last week	two days ago	yesterday morning
last month	two weeks ago	yesterday afternoon
last year	two months ago	yesterday evening
last night	two years ago	the day before yesterday
last Monday	two hours ago	

Note: *This* morning or *this* afternoon can also be a past time expression if you are talking about an earlier time of the day: I *washed* my hair *this morning*.

9 **Write** Answer the questions with a past tense verb and a past time expression.

1. When did you wash your hair? _____ .
2. When did you go shopping? _____ .
3. When did you watch TV? _____ .
4. When did you visit a friend or neighbor? _____ .
5. When did you call your mother? _____ .
6. When did you study? _____ .
7. When did you listen to music? _____ .
8. When did you talk to your teacher the first time? _____ .

10 **Pair Practice** Ask and answer the questions in Activity 9.

11 **Teamwork Task** Work in teams of three. Fill out the chart below for Student 1. Student 1: Answer the questions. Student 2: Choose a time expression from Word Help. Ask Student 1 a question using the time expression (Example: *What did you do last week?*) Student 3: Tell the class about Student 1's past activities. Tell what he or she did and when.

What did you do . . .

TIME EXPRESSION	ACTIVITY
two months ago?	painted my house
_____	_____
_____	_____

Homework

Your Schedule

Make a list of all the things you do in a typical weekend. Change it to the past tense and tell the class everything you did last weekend.

Yesterday

1 **Say It** Practice the conversation with a partner.

get up - got up

A: What time did you <u>get up</u> yesterday?

B: I <u>got up</u> at 7:00. How about you? When did you <u>get up</u>?

A: I <u>got up</u> at 6:30.

Practice the conversation again. Use the pictures below.

1. eat – ate   2. come - came   3. take – took

GRAMMAR CHECK

Past tense irregular

Some past tense verbs don't end in **-ed**. These are irregular verbs. Study the list of irregular verbs below.

2 **Listen** Listen and repeat the present and past of these irregular verbs.

PRESENT	PAST	PRESENT	PAST	PRESENT	PAST
be	was/were	fly	flew	run	ran
begin	began	get	got	say	said
break	broke	give	gave	see	saw
bring	brought	go	went	sell	sold
buy	bought	grow	grew	send	sent
catch	caught	have	had	sing	sang
choose	chose	hear	heard	sleep	slept
cut	cut	know	knew	speak	spoke
do	did	leave	left	swim	swam
draw	drew	make	made	take	took
drink	drank	meet	met	tell	told
drive	drove	pay	paid	wear	wore
fall	fell	read	read	win	won
find	found	ride	rode	write	wrote

> **Note:** Don't add *s* to past tense verbs for *he/she/it*.
> **Correct:** She *ate* chicken yesterday.
> **Incorrect:** She *ates* chicken yesterday.

3 Write Change the present tense sentences to past tense. Include the past time expressions.

HABITUAL	YESTERDAY
1. I eat breakfast every day.	_____ (yesterday)
2. She makes the bed every morning.	_____ (yesterday morning)
3. He drives his car every afternoon.	_____ (yesterday afternoon)
4. I take a shower every night.	_____ (last night)
5. They go to church every Sunday.	_____ (last Sunday)
6. He sleeps eight hours every night.	_____ (last night)
7. She sees her husband every day.	_____ (yesterday)
8. They buy groceries every Saturday.	_____ (last Saturday)

Now write three more sentences of your own using the past tense.

4 Say It Practice the conversation with a partner.

A: Where did you go yesterday?
B: I went to the <u>supermarket</u>.
A: What did you do there?
B: I <u>bought lots of groceries</u>.

supermarket / buy lots of groceries

Practice the conversation again. Use the pictures below.

1. library / meet my friend / read a magazine

2. café / drink coffee / eat a muffin

3. Department of Motor Vehicles / take my driving test

GRAMMAR CHECK

Past tense questions

Use **did** + the present tense verb to form most past tense questions. Use the past tense form for the answer.
Where **did** you **go** yesterday? I **went** to the park.
What **did** you **eat** yesterday? I **ate** a cheeseburger.

5 Write Use the prompts to write the questions.

1. buy / yesterday: _____ What did you buy yesterday _____?

2. see / last night: _____?

3. What time / come to class: _____?

4. What time / class / begin: _____?

5. be / on time for class: _____?

6. eat / yesterday: _____?

7. When / cut / hair: _____?

8. Who / speak to before class: _____?

9. What time / get up this morning: _____?

10. What time / leave / house: _____?

6 Pair Practice Work with a partner.
A. Ask and answer the questions in Activity 5.
B. Student 1—Look at the list of irregular verbs on page 88. Use the verbs from the list to ask your partner ten more questions.

Example: *Student 1:* Where did you **grow** up?
Student 2: I **grew** up in Mexico City.

C. Student 2—Look at the list of irregular verbs on page 88. Use the verbs from the list to ask Student 1 ten more questions. Try not to repeat the same questions, if possible.

7 Group Practice *Find someone who . . .*
Work with a large group or with the whole class. Ask other students questions to find who did the activities below. Write their names.

Example: *Tina:* Did you eat chicken yesterday?
Carlos: No, I didn't.
Tina: Did you buy groceries last week?
Carlos: Yes, I did.

1. _____ ate chicken yesterday.

2. _Carlos_____ bought groceries last week.

3. _____ heard music on the radio yesterday.

4. _____ flew on an airplane last year.

5. _____ brought a pen and a pencil to class.

6. _____ wore blue jeans last week.

7. _____ drove a car yesterday.

8. _____ slept more than eight hours last night.

8 **Teamwork Task** Work in teams of three or four. Imagine what Cindy did yesterday. Did she have a busy day? Fill out her schedule first. Then write as many sentences as you can about what she did in the morning, afternoon, and evening. Choose a team leader to read your story to the class.

	SCHEDULE			
8 AM		**4 PM**	
9 AM	Go to work. Open bakery in supermarket.	**5 PM**	
10 AM		**6 PM**	
11 AM		**7 PM**	
12 AM		**8 PM**	
1 PM		**9 PM**	
2 PM		**10 PM**	
3 PM	Take coffee break.	**11 PM**	

_____

_____

_____

_____

_____

_____

_____

_____

_____

_____

Game Time

What did he or she do?
Your teacher or another student will have (but hide) a picture of something he or she did yesterday or at some point in the past. Or he or she will write a sentence about something he or she did yesterday. Try to guess what it was. *Example:* "Did you watch TV?" "No." "Did you climb a mountain?"

What Did You Do On That Job?

1 Read Read the e-mail from Habib, Jessica's classmate. Circle the past tense verbs.

Hi Jessica!

I got your e-mail yesterday. Thanks for writing. You asked about my job, so I'll tell you about it. I am the manager of a small grocery store. As a manager, I do a lot of different things every day. So, what do I do? Well . . . let me tell you about yesterday since yesterday was a typical day at work for me.

Yesterday morning I started work at 5:15. After I opened the store and turned on the lights, I made a big pot of coffee and put out three dozen donuts on our shelves. I ate one of the donuts, too! I brought in the stacks of newspapers, cut the strings, and placed them on the newspaper rack. Then we were ready for business. We open for business at 5:30.

Yesterday a few people came in right at 5:30. Of course, they wanted coffee. But they bought some other things, too. One customer asked for cold medicine but we don't sell that, so I told her to go to the drugstore around the corner when it opened. At 9:00 my cashier arrived. Then I spoke to the owner. Then I ordered a lot of supplies and groceries.

In the afternoon I talked to more customers, took their money, and gave them change. I left at 3:00 when the night manager showed up. Nobody stole anything. Nobody did anything crazy. It was a typical day at my little grocery store.

Write back soon,
Habib

2 **Write** Write all the past tense verbs from the story in the columns below. Which ones are regular and which are irregular?

REGULAR   IRREGULAR

_____   _____   _____   _____

_____   _____   _____   _____

_____   _____   _____   _____

_____   _____   _____   _____

_____   _____   _____   _____

_____   _____   _____   _____

_____   _____   _____   _____

_____   _____   _____   _____

3 **Pair Practice** Work with a partner. Read Habib's e-mail again. Then ask each other questions about Habib.

Example: *Student 1:*   What time did he start work?
                 Student 2:   He started work at 5:15.
                 Student 2:   What did he turn on at 5:15?
                 Student 1:   He turned on the lights.

4 **Listen** Listen and fill in the blanks in Habib's story.

Habib __got__ his first job in the United States (1)_____ years ago. He
(2)_____ T-shirts and sunglasses from a little stand at the beach. Then
(3)_____ years ago he (4)_____ a man named Sam. Sam (5)_____
him a better job as a clerk in his grocery store. Then (6)_____ years ago
Habib (7)_____ a job as an assistant manager in a larger grocery store.
One year later he (8)_____ the night manager. Then (9)_____
months ago he (10)_____ a big raise and became the store manager.

5 **Pair Practice** Work with a partner. Use the story in Activity 4 to answer the questions.

1. How long ago did Habib get his first job in the United States? _____ .

2. How long ago did Habib sell T-shirts and sunglasses? _____ .

3. How long ago did Habib meet Sam? _____ .

4. How long ago did Habib find an assistant manager position? _____ .

5. How long ago did Habib become a night manager? _____ .

6. How long ago did Habib get a big raise? _____ .

6 **Say It** Practice the conversation with a partner.

A: What was your last job?

B: I was a <u>race car driver</u>.

A: What did you do on that job?

B: I <u>drove fast cars</u> and <u>won races</u>.

A: That sounds exciting!

B: It was.

drive fast cars / win races

Practice the conversation again. Use the pictures below.

1. **write beautiful music /
    sing songs**

2. **hit and catch baseballs /
    run around the bases**

3. **find talented actors and actresses /
    choose actors for TV jobs**

Word Help: Job duties

Job duties are the important tasks you have to do at your job. They usually require knowledge or skills.

Example: A cashier counts money and uses a cash register.
Those tasks are two of his job duties.

7 **Critical Thinking**   What are Habib's job duties? Read Habib's e-mail again. Find the important things he has to do as part of his job.

8 **Match** Match the jobs in Column A with the duties in Column B.

	A		B
_____	1. math teacher	**a.**	answers telephones and greets people
_____	2. pilot	**b.**	teaches mathematics
_____	3. child-care worker	**c.**	fixes cars
_____	4. jockey	**d.**	rides race horses
_____	5. receptionist	**e.**	takes care of sick people
_____	6. nurse	**f.**	takes care of small children
_____	7. auto mechanic	**g.**	cuts and waters grass and flowers
_____	8. gardener	**h.**	flies airplanes
_____	9. plumber	**i.**	takes food orders and serves food
_____	10. waitress/waiter	**j.**	repairs sinks and toilets

9 **Group Practice** Work in groups of five or six. Write a job and its job duties on a piece of paper. Pretend it was your last job. (You can use a real job you had or one of the jobs from this chapter.) Ask your classmates what their last job was, and what their duties were on that job. Remember to answer in the past tense.

NAME	JOB	WHAT HE/SHE DID
_____	_____	_____
_____	_____	_____
_____	_____	_____
_____	_____	_____
_____	_____	_____

Culture Tip

How many jobs?

American workers today have to be flexible. The average worker changes jobs every three years in the U.S. How often do people change jobs in your part of this country or in your home country?

10 **Group Practice** Work in groups of three or four. Look at the list below of important things that can change a person's life. Choose five things that change a person's life the most. Talk about them. Tell the other students your opinions. Your group can choose only five things. You have to agree on which five to choose.

* Finish school	_____	* Learn English	_____
* Get married	_____	* Get a driver's license	_____
* Move to a new country	_____	* Get a good job (good pay)	_____
* Get your first job	_____	* Get divorced	_____
* Have a child	_____	* Vote for the first time	_____
* Buy a house	_____	* Buy a car	_____

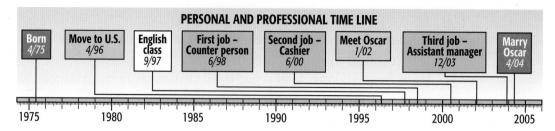

PERSONAL AND PROFESSIONAL TIME LINE

Born 4/75 | Move to U.S. 4/96 | English class 9/97 | First job – Counter person 6/98 | Second job – Cashier 6/00 | Meet Oscar 1/02 | Third job – Assistant manager 12/03 | Marry Oscar 4/04

1975   1980   1985   1990   1995   2000   2005

11 **Write** Use the time line to answer the questions about Laura Lee. Write complete sentences. Use *ago* in your answers.

1. When was Laura born? <u>She was born   years ago   </u>.

2. When did she come to the U.S.? _____.

3. When did she take her first English class? _____.

4. When did she get her first job? _____.

5. When did she meet Oscar? _____.

6. When did she become an assistant manager? _____.

12 **Problem Solving** Use the time line to answer the questions about Laura.

1. How old is Laura now? _____.

2. How old was she when she moved to the U.S.? _____.

3. How old was she when she got her first job? _____.

4. How long did she work as a counter person? _____.

5. How long did she work as a cashier? _____.

6. How long did she know Oscar before she married him? _____.

13 **Pair Practice** Create a time line for your life. Think about the five or six most important events of your life. Write the events and the dates on the time line below. Then tell your partner about your life.

1975   1980   1985   1990   1995   2000   2005

Homework

Time Line

Create a time line for someone in your family or for a friend. Write the most important things in his or her life and the dates they happened. Then tell the class about the person.

1 Read and Listen Read the story. Then listen to the story. Circle the past tense verbs.

Jessica's Interesting Day

Jessica had a very interesting day last Saturday. In the afternoon she rode her bicycle to the beach. It was a warm, sunny day, so when she got to the beach she stopped at an outdoor café. She took out her pen and started to draw. She drew a picture of the beach with the palm trees in the front and the ocean in the background. She added a young couple talking near one of the palm trees. When she finished, she heard a man's voice over her shoulder. "That's beautiful," he said. "You are very talented." She smiled.

They talked about art for a while. His name was Jack. He knew a lot about art. And he was very nice, too. She enjoyed talking to him. Later, when Jessica left the café, she passed an art gallery around the corner. The paintings in the window were very good so she decided to go in. She walked slowly around the gallery and looked at each picture for a long time. Then she heard Jack's voice again. "I hope you like them," he said. "They're mine." He told her he was an artist, but he also worked as the art director of a computer animation company. "Really? Jessica said. "I work for a computer animation company, too."

Later, he offered to drive her home.

"No, thanks," she said. "I have my bicycle here."

"I enjoyed talking to you," he said. "Would you like to give me your phone number so we can talk again some time?"

She thought about it for a few seconds. "No," she said, "I don't think so."

"OK," he said, "but, please, take my card."

He gave her his business card. She got on her bicycle. She put the card into her shirt pocket.

2 Write Write the answers to the questions.

1. How did Jessica get to the beach? _____ .

2. Where did she stop at the beach? _____ .

3. What did she draw? _____ .

4. How long did Jack and Jessica talk about art? _____ .

5. Why did Jessica go into the gallery? _____ .

6. Did Jack drive Jessica home? _____ .

7. What did he give her? _____ .

CRITICAL THINKING:

8. Do you think Jessica should call Jack? Why or why not?

_____

_____

3 Write Write about an interesting day you had. When was it? Where did you go? What did you do? What happened?

_____

_____

_____

_____

_____

4 Best Answer Bubble the correct answer.   a   b   c

1. She ate dinner _____ .

   a) last night   **b)** every night   **c)** tonight   ○   ○   ○

2. He _____ a car last year.

   a) buy   **b)** bought   **c)** have   ○   ○   ○

3. She went to the beach three days _____ .

   a) last   **b)** before   **c)** ago   ○   ○   ○

4. He _____ lunch at 1:30.

   a) took   **b)** eat   **c)** had   ○   ○   ○

5. She _____ her house at 6:30.

   a) leave   **b)** leaved   **c)** left   ○   ○   ○

5 **Write** Look at the picture. What did everybody do at James and Laura's barbecue last night? Write sentences below.

1. James _____.
2. Eric _____.
3. Laura and Jessica _____.
4. Lin and Alex _____.
5. Habib _____.
6. Tania _____.
7. Cindy and Alberto _____.
8. Oscar _____.

6 **Write** Complete the dialogue with information about yourself.

A: How _____ your weekend?

B: _____. On Saturday _____.

A: What _____ you _____ after that?

B: After that, _____ and then _____.

A: Sounds like an interesting day. What time _____ you _____ up on Sunday?

B: I _____.

A: What time did you come to class today?

B: I _____.

7 **Teamwork Task** Work in teams of three or four. Choose a volunteer (Student 1) from your team and create a time line for that person. Include as much information as possible. Student 2: Ask personal information questions. Student 3: Ask professional information questions. Write the information on the time line below. Then tell the class about your teammate's life. (Remember to use past tense verbs!)

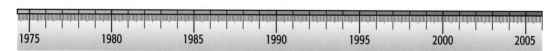

1975   1980   1985   1990   1995   2000   2005

8 **Teamwork Task** Work in teams of three. Find someone in the school or community to interview as a group. Student 1: Ask personal information questions. Student 2: Ask professional information questions. Write the information on the time line below. Student 3: Tell the class about the life of this person. Remember to use past tense verbs!

Pronunciation Past tense endings with the sounds *t*, *d*, and *id*. You will hear a list of nine verbs. Listen carefully to the past tense verb endings. Write each past tense verb in the correct column.

SOUNDS LIKE *t*	SOUNDS LIKE *d*	SOUNDS LIKE *id*
watched		

INTERNET IDEA: Research
Pick a famous person. Do research on that person on the Internet. Use a search engine to help you find the information. Create a personal and professional time line for that person and write a paragraph about his or her life. Present your time line and information to the class.

I can . . .			
• talk about past events.	1	2	3
• compare today with yesterday.	1	2	3
• use verbs in the past tense.	1	2	3
• ask and answer past tense questions.	1	2	3
• create a team story.	1	2	3
• describe a sequence of past events.	1	2	3
• describe past job duties.	1	2	3
• interpret a time line.	1	2	3
• create a personal and professional time line.	1	2	3

1 = not well   2 = OK   3 = very well

DOWNTOWN

9 **Write** Write the missing words in the cartoon story. Use the past tense of these verbs: *get, drive, crush, buy, see, come, fall (2), find, fly, lose, happen, leave.*

Cindy: So, how was your day?
Alberto: It was terrible.
Cindy: Why? What (1)_____?

Alberto: First, I didn't hear my alarm clock and I (2)_____ up late. Then I (3)_____ too fast and I got a speeding ticket.
Cindy: Oh no!

Alberto: Then, I (4)_____ my wallet in the supermarket.
Cindy: Did you find it?
Alberto: Fortunately, the manager (5)_____ it.

Alberto: After that, I (6)_____ a box of chocolates for an after dinner treat.
Cindy: And?
Alberto: I (7)_____ it on top of my car, then it (8)_____ off and another car (9)_____ it!

Alberto: But then I (10)_____ here and (11)_____ you.
Cindy: And?

Cindy: And?
Alberto: And all my troubles (12)_____ out the window.
Cindy: I'm glad. But look! My plant just (13)_____ out the window, too!

10 **Pair Practice** Practice the cartoon story with a partner.

Free Time

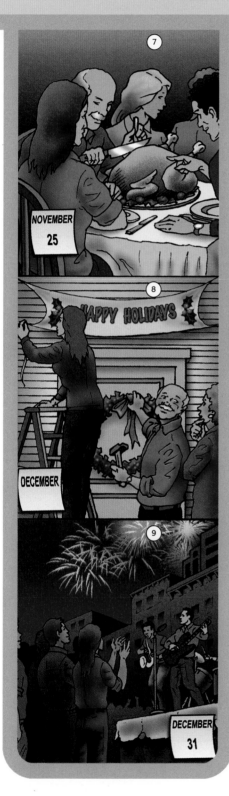

1 Read and Listen *Look at the pictures and read the story. Then listen to the story below. Complete the chart.*

Holidays

Jessica enjoyed the holidays during her first year in the United States. She went skiing at Big Bear Mountain on New Year's Day. She went hiking and camping on Memorial Day. She went swimming at Malibu Beach on Independence Day. And of course, she went dancing on Valentine's Day. During spring break, she went sightseeing in San Francisco. That was a lot of fun.

She also went to some nice holiday parties and events. On Halloween she went to a costume party, and on Thanksgiving she went to a family party at her aunt's house. She also helped decorate her aunt's house for the holidays in December. And on New Year's Eve she had a great time at the street festival. She saw a concert and a fireworks show. She is looking forward to some more enjoyable holidays next year.

DATE	HOLIDAY	WHAT DID SHE DO?

How Was Your Vacation?

1 **Say It** Practice the conversation with a partner.

camping? hiking

A: How was your vacation?

B: It was great.

A: Where did you go?

B: I went to <u>Yosemite National Park</u>.

A: Did you go <u>camping</u> there?

B: No, I didn't. I went <u>hiking</u>.

Practice the conversation again. Use the pictures below.

1. fishing? swimming

2. dancing? sightseeing

3. horseback riding?
   water skiing

Note: **Go + gerund**

We use *go* and a gerund (the *-ing* form of a verb) to describe many recreation or free-time activities.

Correct: We go **dancing** a lot.

Incorrect: We go *to dancing* a lot.

Word Help: Here are some activities we usually identify with *go* and a gerund:

go shopping	go dancing	go horseback riding
go bike riding	go swimming	go jogging (running)
go hiking	go (water) skiing	go fishing
go (ice) skating	go camping	go sailing

2 **Pair Practice** Free-time activities
  A. Put a check next to the free-time activities you sometimes do.
  B. Check which activities you did last year.
  C. Ask your partner which activities he or she sometimes does.
  D. Check which activities he or she did last year.
  E. Add any other activities in the blank spaces at the end of the chart.

	YOU		YOUR PARTNER	
	DO YOU SOMETIMES . . . ?	DID YOU . . . LAST YEAR?	DO YOU SOMETIMES . . . ?	DID YOU . . . LAST YEAR?
1. go swimming				
2. go dancing				
3. go hiking				
4. eat in a good restaurant				
5. play a sport				
6. play cards				
7. go jogging				
8. ride a horse				
9. take photographs				
10. buy souvenirs				
11. sunbathe				
12. go sightseeing				
13. go windowshopping				
14. have a picnic				
15.				
16.				

Note: *And* or *but*?
  Use *and* when two parts of a sentence agree.
  Use *but* when they disagree.
Examples: I sleep late, **and** he sleeps late, too.
  I often go jogging, **but** he doesn't (go jogging).

3 **Write** On a separate piece of paper, write three sentences about things you and your partner both like to do. Write three sentences about things you and your partner both did last year. Write three sentences where you and your partner disagree.

Short answers in the simple past

Question	Positive Answer	Negative Answer
Did you come to class yesterday?	Yes, I **did**.	No, I **didn't. (did not)**
Did he come to class yesterday?	Yes, he **did**.	No, he **didn't. (did not)**
Did they come to class yesterday?	Yes, they **did**.	No, they **didn't. (did not)**

Check Point: Negative

✓ Use *did not (didn't)* + base form of the verb to make a negative sentence:
Example: Did you get up early?
Correct: No, I **didn't get** up early. I **didn't have** to go to work.
Incorrect: No, I *didn't got* up early.

④ Pair Practice Work with a partner. Look at the pictures on page 102. Ask and answer *yes/no* questions about Jessica's holiday activities last year.

Example: *Student 1:* Did Jessica go skiing on New Year's Day?
Student 2: Yes, she did.
Student 2: Did she go swimming on Valentine's Day?
Student 1: No, she didn't.

⑤ Group Practice Work in a large group or with the whole class. Write on a piece of paper one free-time activity you did last year. Walk around the class and ask five other students short answer questions about their activity.

Example: *Student 1:* Did you have a picnic last year?
Student 2: No, I didn't.
Student 1: Did you take photographs last year?
Student 2: Yes, I did.

⑥ Say It Practice the conversation with a partner.

play volleyball?
go jogging?

A: Would you like to <u>play volleyball</u> today?
B: No, thanks. I <u>played volleyball</u> yesterday.
A: Would you like to <u>go jogging</u>?
B: No, thanks. I <u>went jogging</u> two days ago.
A: Would you like to <u>go dancing</u>?
B: Yes, I'd love to.

Practice more conversations. Use the pictures below.

1. have a picnic?
    go swimming?

2. take photographs?
    buy souvenirs?

3. go sightseeing?
    go shopping?

7 Write Write about a vacation you took in the past. It can be true or not true.

1. How was your vacation? _____ .
2. Where did you go? _____ .
3. How long did you stay? _____ .
4. How did you get there? _____ .
5. What did you eat /drink? _____ .
6. When did you go? _____ .
7. What did you do there? _____ .

8 Pair Practice Work with a partner. Ask and answer the questions in Activity 7.

WORD HELP: Seasons

Spring:
March 21-June 20

Summer:
June 21 – September 22

Fall:
September 23-
December 21

Winter:
December 22-March 20

9 Teamwork Task Work in teams of three or four. Make a list of interesting places to go on vacation. When is the best time of year to go there? What can you do there? Write about as many places as you can. Present your chart to the class.

PLACE	SEASON	WHAT YOU CAN DO THERE

How Was the Weather?

1 Listen Listen to the national weather report. Write the missing temperatures on the map.

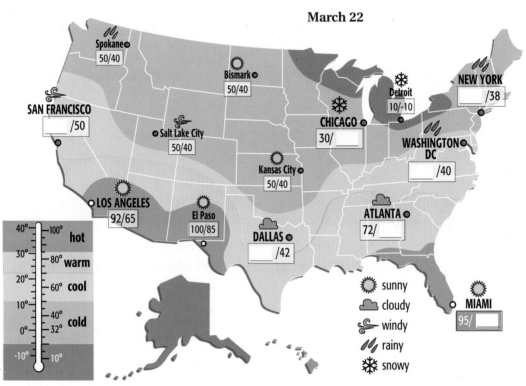

March 22

Spokane 50/40

Bismark 50/40

Detroit 10/-10

NEW YORK /38

SAN FRANCISCO /50

Salt Lake City 50/40

CHICAGO 30/

WASHINGTON DC /40

Kansas City 50/40

LOS ANGELES 92/65

El Paso 100/85

ATLANTA 72/

DALLAS /42

sunny
cloudy
windy
rainy
snowy

40° — 100° hot
30° — 80° warm
20° — 60° cool
10° — 40° cold
0° — 32°
-10° — 10°

MIAMI 95/

2 Write Answer the questions about the weather map.

1. What was the high temperature in Miami? _____ .

2. What was the weather like in New York? _____ .

3. Which city was the coldest? _____ .

4. What was the weather like in Atlanta? _____ .

5. What was the low temperature in Chicago? _____ .

6. How was the weather in San Francisco? _____ .

7. Which city was the hottest? _____ .

8. What season of the year is it? _____ .

9. Which city would you like to be in? Why? _____

_____ .

> **Note: How is the weather?**
> We usually use a form of *be* + positive adjectives for warm and dry weather.
>
> The weather **is** nice, or great, or beautiful.
>
> We usually use a form of *be* + negative adjectives for cold or wet weather.
>
> The weather **is** bad, or terrible, or awful.

3 **Say It** Practice the conversation with a partner.

A: Where did you go last weekend?

B: I went to <u>Boston</u>.

A: How was the weather there?

B: It was <u>awful</u>. It was <u>cold and rainy</u> all weekend.

A: What was the temperature?

B: It was about <u>forty degrees</u>.

Practice the conversation again. Use the pictures below.

1

2

3

4 **Group Practice** Work in groups of five or six.

A. Choose a city on the weather map on page 108. Write your name on the place. Pretend you were there last weekend.

B. Ask the other students in your group where they went last weekend and what the weather was like there.

Culture Tip

Small Talk

Small talk is conversation that isn't very personal or important. People often talk about the weather as a topic of "small talk." Its purpose is just to make people feel comfortable. What other topics might be "small talk"?

Listen Listen to the conversation. Write the weather and temperature you hear for each city.

CITY	WEATHER	TEMPERATURE
London		
Paris		
Mexico City		
Tokyo		
Barcelona		

GRAMMAR CHECK

Short answers: *did* vs. *was/were*

Question Word	Short Answer	Example Sentence
Did	**did** or **didn't**	Did you have a nice Thanksgiving? Yes, I **did**. *OR* No, I **didn't**.
Was/Were	**was/were** *OR* **wasn't/weren't**	Were you home last night? Yes, I **was**.

Check Point:
✓ Remember that short answers should match the question.

6 **Write** Fill in the blanks with short answers or question words.

1. Did Jessica go to San Francisco last April?   Yes, ____ ____ .
2. Was it windy in San Francisco in April?   Yes, ____ ____ .
3. Did Jessica go swimming in January?   No, ____ ____ .
4. Was the weather cold on the 4th of July?   No, ____ ____ .
5. Were Jessica's classmates in New York last month?   No, ____ ____ .
6. ____ Jessica and Victor go dancing on February 14?   <u>Yes,</u> <u>they</u> <u>did</u> .
7. ____ it windy on July 4th?   <u>No,</u> <u>it</u> <u>wasn't.</u>
8. ____ you in London last summer?   ____ , ____ .
9. ____ you go to San Francisco last month?   ____ , ____ .
10. ____ it hot in Las Vegas in July?   Yes, it _____ .

7 **Pair Practice** Work with a partner. Ask and answer the questions in Activity 6.

8 **Say It** Practice the conversation with a partner.

go to Mexico?

A: Did you <u>go to Mexico</u> on your last vacation?

B: No, we didn't <u>go to Mexico</u>.

A: <u>Where did you go?</u>

B: <u>We went to Yosemite</u>.

A: Did you have a good time?

B: Yes, we did.

Practice the conversation again. Use the pictures below.

1. see the Golden Gate Bridge?

2. take a bus?

3. have good weather?

9 **Write** Write about the vacations below. Write one negative and one positive sentence for each number. Use the cues to help you.

AT HOME	ON VACATION
1. Angela usually cooks dinner. (restaurant)	*She didn't cook dinner* . *She ate in a restaurant* .
2. Alex usually takes a shower in the morning. (afternoon and evening)	_____ . _____ .
3. Jessica usually gets up early. (about 9:30)	_____ . _____ .
4. Rosa usually buys groceries. (souvenirs)	_____ . _____ .
5. Alex usually works all day. (rest and relax)	_____ . _____ .

⑩ Group Practice Work in groups of five. Tell the group about a place you visited in the United States or in your country. Tell the name of the place and when you went there. Other students in your group will ask questions about your trip using *Was/Were . . . ?* and *Did . . . ?*

Example: *Student 2:* How was the weather there?
Student 1: It was hot and sunny.
Student 3: Did you take a lot of pictures?
Student 1: Yes, I did.

⑪ Teamwork Task Work in teams of three or four. Prepare a weather report for the class. Choose three or four of the cities on the map, one for each team member. If you want to make the weather severe, use words in the Word Help box. Present your weather report to the class.

WORD HELP:

drought: a long period of little or no rain

sandstorm: a strong wind blowing sand through the air, usually happening in the desert

blizzard: a very heavy snowstorm with strong winds

hurricane: a powerful storm that is 200 to 300 miles in diameter; winds at its center are 75 miles or more

tornado: a moving column of air, shaped like an upside-down funnel with very strong winds—over 500 miles per hour

mud slide: caused by heavy rains; can happen on the California coast

PLACE	WEATHER

I Work at a Travel Agency

1 **Read** Read the e-mail from Jessica's friend Debbie. Circle and count the past tense verbs. Discuss the vocabulary with your teacher.

Hi Jessica!

It was nice to hear from you down there in L.A. It's sunny today, and Seattle is really beautiful on sunny days. Unfortunately, there aren't very many of them! Your job sounds great. I have a really good job, too. I'm working as a travel agent. I'm learning all about the travel industry. I can travel anywhere in the world for a really low price. Last month I got a free trip to a resort in Cancún, Mexico. I stayed there three nights. I slept late every morning and ate a big breakfast at 10:00. Then I swam in the pool and played tennis in the afternoon. I took dancing lessons at 5:00 every day. And then after dinner I went dancing at the disco where I met some very nice people!

I know that doesn't sound like work, so you're probably wondering what I actually do on my job. Well, yesterday I sold tours to six people. I also sent one young couple to Paris. I found a great air/hotel deal for $150 a night. I booked cruises for two couples. And I made airline reservations for ten other customers. So, I actually did a lot.

As a matter of fact, I have to go back to work right now. So, take care. And write again soon.

Debbie

2 **Write** Read the sentences. Circle True or False.

1. Debbie likes her job.	True	False
2. Debbie is a travel agent.	True	False
3. Debbie slept until 11:00 in Cancún.	True	False
4. Debbie can travel anywhere in the world for free.	True	False
5. Yesterday Debbie went to Paris.	True	False
6. Yesterday Debbie booked cruises for four people.	True	False

CRITICAL THINKING:

7. I would like Debbie's job.	True	False

Why? or Why not?

3 **Say It** Practice the conversation with a partner.

A: Hi. This is Debbie. How can I help you?

B: I'm interested in going to <u>Hawaii</u>. Do you have any specials?

A: Yes, we do. We have a <u>three-night special at the Beachfront Hotel for $500 per person</u>.

B: Does that include airfare?

A: Yes, it does.

B: Are there any discounts?

A: <u>Yes. There is a 10% discount if you book it before August 15</u>.

B: That sounds great. I'd like to book it.

Practice the conversation again. Use the ads below.

Culture Tip

Travel and Tourism

Travel and tourism is one of the largest industries in the United States. The United States is the second most popular country to visit: 42 million international visitors traveled to the U.S. in 2003 and spent $72 billion. France is the most popular country to visit. What country would you like to visit?

④ Listen Listen and write the missing numbers in the train schedule.

SILVERSTREAK 1		BOSTON to NEW YORK	SCENIC CRUISER 1		BOSTON to NEW YORK
Departs BOSTON	8:30 AM		Departs BOSTON	9:00 AM	
Arrives NEW YORK	12:25 PM	**One-Way** $55	Arrives NEW YORK	☐	**One-Way** $39
Departs NEW YORK	2:45 PM		Departs NEW YORK	☐	
Arrives WASHINGTON, D.C.	☐	**Round-Trip** $98	Arrives WASHINGTON, D.C.	8:20 PM	**Round-Trip** $69

SILVERSTREAK 2		BOSTON to WASHINGTON	SCENIC CRUISER 2		BOSTON to WASHINGTON
Departs BOSTON	☐		Departs BOSTON	11:00 AM	
Arrives NEW YORK	5:50 PM	**One-Way** $79	Arrives NEW YORK	☐	**One-Way** $45
Departs NEW YORK	7:00 PM		Departs NEW YORK	6:00 PM	
Arrives WASHINGTON, D.C.	☐	**Round-Trip** ☐	Arrives WASHINGTON, D.C.	12:15 AM	**Round-Trip** ☐

GRAMMAR CHECK

Simple present tense for scheduled future events

We use the simple present tense to talk about scheduled events that take place in the future. You will learn the future tense in Chapter 7.

Example: What time **does** the train leave for New York tonight?
It **leaves** at 8:00. (*Not:* It *will leave* at 8:00.)

⑤ Say It Practice the conversation with a partner.

BOSTON – NEW YORK (RT)

SCENIC CRUISER 1
(too late)

SILVERSTREAK 1

A: Fast Track. How can I help you?

B: I'd like to go from <u>Boston</u> to <u>New York</u> tomorrow.

A: One-way or round-trip?

B: <u>Round-trip</u>, please.

A: OK. We have the <u>Scenic Cruiser 1</u> that leaves <u>Boston</u> at <u>9:00 A.M.</u> and arrives in <u>New York</u> at <u>2:05 P.M.</u>

B: That's <u>too late</u>.

A: We also have the <u>Silverstreak 1</u> that leaves <u>Boston</u> at <u>8:30 A.M.</u> and arrives in <u>New York</u> at <u>12:25 P.M.</u>

B: That sounds good. How much is it?

A: One <u>round-trip</u> ticket is <u>$98</u>.

Practice the conversation again. Use the chart on page 115 and the cues below.

BOSTON-WASHINGTON, D.C. (One-Way)
SCENIC CRUISER 1
(too early)
SCENIC CRUISER 2

1

BOSTON-NEW YORK (One-Way)
SILVERSTREAK 1
(too early)
SILVERSTREAK 2

2

BOSTON-WASHINGTON, D.C. (RT)
SILVERSTREAK 1
(too early)
SCENIC CRUISER 1

3

6 **Read** Read the graph about Debbie's Cancún Tour. What were the most popular activities? The least popular?

❶ Swim in the ocean	❷ Play volleyball	❸ Take dance lessons	❹ Go hiking	❺ Sunbathe at the pool	❻ Dance in disco	❼ Eat at beach barbecue	❽ Drink cold drinks at the bar	❾ Stay in hotel room

7 **Pair Practice** Work with a partner. Ask and answer questions about Debbie's Cancún Tour. Remember to use past tense verbs!

Example:　*Student 1:*　How many people played volleyball?
　　　　　　　Student 2:　Eight people played volleyball.

8 **Teamwork Task** Work in teams of three. You work at a travel agency. Plan a tour of an interesting place. Work together to make a list of six to eight activities for people to do on your tour. Do research on the Internet or in the library if needed. Student 1: Create the list. Student 2: Do a class survey of the whole class. Ask how many students would like to do each of the activities. Student 3: Write the numbers for each activity on the graph. Work together to create a graph like Debbie's Cancún Tour graph.

Write sentences about how many people did each of the activities on your tour.

Game Time

What did he or she do?
Choose a classmate. This classmate will write an activity that he or she did on his or her vacation. Close your books and ask yes/no questions. Try to guess what your classmate did. Play again with another classmate.

1 Read Read the story. Try to guess which verbs are missing.

Vacations

Several of Jessica's classmates _____ interesting vacations last year. Her friend Lin took a vacation in the fall. She _____ to the Grand Canyon in Arizona for three days. The weather _____ great. The temperature was 75° during the day and 55° at night. The views in the Grand Canyon _____ fantastic. She went hiking and camping but she _____ _____ fishing. She doesn't like fishing very much. She does like horseback riding very much. One afternoon she _____ a horse next to the Colorado River for several hours. That was her favorite part of the trip.

Jessica's friend Alex took his vacation in the winter. He went to Florida for a week. He _____ in Orlando for the first two days. Then he _____ down to Miami. He saw a lot of beautiful places along the way. He _____ in the ocean in Daytona Beach and again in Ft. Lauderdale. In Miami he went to nightclubs and danced and danced. He _____ a lot of friendly and interesting people there.

Elham and her husband, Hamed, _____ to save some money, so they _____ at home for their vacation. They _____ late, _____ to the library, _____ a few movies, and _____ at a new restaurant. The weather was nice so they _____ some gardening and _____ for walks in different neighborhoods. They also _____ their apartment. They _____ a great time and felt relaxed. And they _____ have to unpack a suitcase at the end of their vacation!

2 Listen and Write Listen to the story. Write the verbs you hear in the blanks.

3 Write Answer the questions with complete sentences.

1. How were the views at the Grand Canyon? _____ .

2. Why didn't Lin go fishing? _____ .

3. Where did Lin ride a horse? _____ .

4. What did Alex do in Miami? _____ .

5. Why did Elham and Hamed stay at home for their vacation? _____ .

6. What did they do during their vacation? _____ .

CRITICAL THINKING:

7. Which vacation do you think was the best? Why? _____ .

_____ .

4 Best Answer Bubble the correct answer.   a   b   c

1. What did you do on vacation? I _____ in the pool.

   a) went swam   b) swimming   c) went swimming   ○   ○   ○

2. She went hiking, _____ she didn't go fishing.

   a) and   b) but   c) so   ○   ○   ○

3. Independence Day in the U.S. is in the _____.

   a) summer   b) winter   c) spring   ○   ○   ○

4. Jessica likes to go _____.

   a) dance   b) listen to music c) shopping   ○   ○   ○

5. Did you go back to Columbia last year? No, I didn't _____.

   a) went   b) go   c) going   ○   ○   ○

5 Write Complete the conversation with information about yourself. (You can use real information or you can pretend.)

A: How was your vacation?   A: How long did you stay?

B: _____ .   B: _____ .

A: Where did you go?   A: What did you do there?

B: _____ .   B: _____ .

A: How was the weather?   A: What else did you do?

B: _____ .   B: _____ .

A: What was the temperature?   A: Did you have a good time?

B: _____ .   B: _____ .

6 Pair Practice Work with a partner. Practice the conversation in Activity 5 with your partner.

7 Write Look at the pictures of Tania and Dina's vacation. Under each picture write a question. Then write a positive and negative answer connected by *but*. The first one is done for you.

Last year Tania and Dina went on vacation together. Tania was energetic and felt great. She wanted to do everything. Dina had a cold. She was tired and didn't feel well. She didn't want to do anything.

Did they play tennis?   _____   _____

Tania played tennis, but   _____   _____

Dina didn't.   _____   _____

_____ _____ _____

_____ _____ _____

_____ _____ _____

8 **Teamwork Task**

A. Work in teams of four or five. Work together to create an ad for a holiday vacation in New York City. Use the ad box below. Include how many days/nights, the cost of the vacation, the hotel or resort, the travel dates, any discounts, and the name and phone number of the travel agent.

B. Student 1: You are the tourist. Call the travel agent. Ask questions and make a reservation for the New York City vacation.

C. Student 2: You are the travel agent. Answer the questions and make reservations for the vacation. (Don't forget to ask the tourist his or her name and credit card number.)

D. Student 3: You are the tour director for the New York City Vacation Tour. Make a list of activities for your tour group. (Ask your teammates to help you.)

E. Student 4: Tell the class about your team's vacation to New York City. Tell how many nights the vacation lasts, the cost of the vacation, and what activities will be available.

Pronunciation Reduction: *Didjuh* instead of *did you*

Many native speakers join words together when they speak. They make two words sound like one word. Native speakers often say *didjuh* instead of *did you*.

A. Listen and repeat the following sentences.

Where did you go?

Did you go to New York?

What did you do there?

Did you have a good time?

B. Work with a partner. Ask your partner some questions with *Did you . . . ?* Say *didjuh* instead of *did you*.

INTERNET IDEA

Travel

Go on the Internet to find a travel Web site. Find a place you would like to visit. Try to find a vacation tour package for that place. How many days is it? How much does it cost? What dates is the package available?

I can . . .			
• identify common U.S. holidays.	1	2	3
• talk about free-time activities.	1	2	3
• offer, decline, and accept invitations.	1	2	3
• understand a weather map.	1	2	3
• talk about the weather.	1	2	3
• write about a past vacation.	1	2	3
• read transportation schedules.	1	2	3
• read travel ads.	1	2	3
• plan a vacation.	1	2	3
• ask and respond to yes/no past tense questions.	1	2	3

1 = not well   2 = OK   3 = very well

DOWNTOWN

9 Write Write the missing words in the cartoon story. Use these words: *It, cried, leave, was, Did, went, took, met, left, ate, swam, dove.*

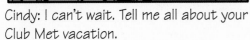

Cindy: I can't wait. Tell me all about your Club Met vacation.
Rosa: Well, first of all, the location (1)_____ really perfect. (2)_____ was hot in the afternoon and warm enough to swim at night.

Cindy: (3)_____ you swim at night?
Rosa: I (4)_____ every morning, afternoon, and night. And, as you can see, I (5)_____ a lot of pictures on the beach.

Cindy: Who is this handsome guy?
Rosa: That's Billy. I (6)_____ him the night I arrived. For three days we (7)_____ hiking, swimming, and sailing together.

Rosa: We (8)_____ breakfast, lunch, and dinner together.
Cindy: You did?
Rosa: He even (9)_____ into the ocean to get me this beautiful seashell as a souvenir.
Cindy: That's so romantic!

Rosa: And then on the last day, he (10)_____. He didn't (11)_____ me his phone number. He didn't even say goodbye.
Cindy: Oh, Rosa, that's terrible!

Rosa: I (12)_____ for three hours. But you know what, Cindy?
Cindy: What?
Rosa: There are a lot more shells in the sea!

10 Pair Practice Practice the cartoon story with a partner.

Shopping

GOALS

- ✓ Identify sections of a department store
- ✓ Ask for and give locations
- ✓ Interpret a bar graph
- ✓ Make predictions using *will* or *won't*
- ✓ Talk about future possibilities
- ✓ Rank people and things using superlative adjectives
- ✓ Describe product defects
- ✓ Return or exchange an item
- ✓ Understand advertisements
- ✓ Compare ads
- ✓ Fill out a credit application

CHAPTER 7

1 **Read and Listen** *Look at the picture of the department store. Read Jessica's story. Then listen to her story.*

Shopping Plans

It is a week before the winter holidays. Jessica and Dulce are going to the big sale at the Downtown Department Store. Dulce wants to go to the men's department. She will probably buy a shirt for her dad. Then she'll go to the jewelry department to get something for her mom. She might buy a pair of earrings or she might buy a nice necklace. Or she might buy her some perfume in the cosmetics department. Then she'll go alone to the entertainment section where she'll buy a CD for Jessica.

Jessica will go to the electronics department where she might buy a portable CD player for her uncle, if it isn't too expensive. She probably won't go to the toy section, but she will definitely go to the housewares section to get a toaster for her aunt. And she'll go to sporting goods where she might get a fishing rod for her cousin, Martin. She won't look at the stoves in the appliance section. She will go to Customer Service to return a shirt that's too big. Then she'll go to the women's department and look for a cute sweater for Dulce. She might look for a cute shirt for herself, but she probably won't buy it. She probably won't have any money left!

Write the names of the departments in the store directory.

STORE DIRECTORY	
FIRST FLOOR:	**SECOND FLOOR**
1. _____	6. _____
2. _____	7. _____
3. _____	8. _____
4. _____	9. _____
5. _____	10. _____
	11. _____

Where Can I Find the Pots and Pans?

1 **Say It** Practice the conversation with a partner.

pots and pans?

A: Excuse me. Where can I find the <u>pots and pans</u>, please?

B: <u>They're</u> in the <u>housewares</u> department.

A: Where is that?

B: The <u>housewares</u> department is on the first floor, <u>in the back near the shoe department</u>.

A: Thank you.

Practice the conversation again. Use the pictures below.

1. perfume?

2. bicycles?

3. sofas?

Word Help: Locations

1. It's in the front.

2. It's in the back.

3. It's on the right.

4. It's on the left.

2 **Pair Practice** Work with a partner. Look at the picture of the department store on page 122. Ask about the location of other things in the department store.

Example: *Student 1:* Where are the tennis racquets?
Student 2: They're in the sporting goods department. That's on the second floor on the left near . . .

JESSICA'S CLASSMATES: *Where will they shop this year?*

Men's	13
Women's	19
Jewelry	6
Cosmetics	14
Electronics	8
Sporting goods	4
Furniture	3
Toys	8

3 **Pair Practice** Work with a partner. Ask and answer questions about Jessica's classmates.

Example: *Student 1:* How many of Jessica's classmates will buy something in the men's department this year?

Student 2: Thirteen people will buy something in the men's department this year.

4 **Group Practice** Work in groups of ten, or with the whole class. Do a class or group survey. Ask how many people will shop at each of the departments this year. On a separate piece of paper, use the numbers to create a bar graph for your group. Fill in the columns with pencils or markers.

OUR CLASSMATES: *Where will we shop this year?*

Men's
Women's
Jewelry
Cosmetics
Electronics
Sporting goods
Furniture
Toys
Entertainment

Future—*Will*

Positive		I/you/he/she/it/we/they	**will arrive** tomorrow.
Negative		I/you/he/she/it/we/they	**won't (will not)** arrive tomorrow.
Question	**Will**	I/you/he/she/it/we/they	arrive tomorrow?
Short answers	Yes,	I/you/he/she/it/we/they	**will.**
	No,		**won't.**

Check Point:

  ✓ Use *will* + verb to form the future.

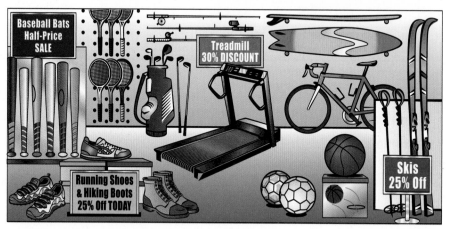

5   **Write**   What will Jessica's classmates buy next summer? Write one positive and one negative sentence about each of Jessica's classmates.

1. Lin likes hiking, but she doesn't like fishing at all.

   <u>I think she will buy . . .</u>   .

   <u>She won't buy . . .</u>   .

2. Alex loves skiing, but he hates baseball.

   _____ .

   _____ .

3. Tania likes running, but she doesn't like basketball.

   _____ .

   _____ .

4. Hong Yu likes tennis, but she hates running.

   _____ .

   _____ .

5. Manuel loves to play soccer, but he doesn't like golf at all.

   _____ .

   _____ .

6 **Pair Practice** Predictions. Work with a partner. Answer the questions with your own opinions.

Example: *Student 1:* How many students will come to class tomorrow?
              Student 2: I think twelve students will come to class.

1. What will your teacher wear to class tomorrow?

2. How will the weather be tomorrow?

3. What time will you get up tomorrow?

4. When will you go to the supermarket?

5. How much money will you spend tomorrow?

6. Where will you be five years from now?

7 **Teamwork Task** Work in teams of three or four. Look at the picture. Work together to write a future story about the picture. Make predictions about what will happen to these people in the future. Use *will* in your sentences. Write as many future sentences as you can about the people in the picture. Answer questions such as: Will they get married? Where will they live? Will they be happy? What else will happen? What will the girl's parents say or do?

Game Time

What will they buy?

1. On a piece of paper write the name of a department in a department store (Electronics, Men's, etc.). Then write something you want to buy from that department. Don't let other students see it.

2. Go to the front of the room. Write your department on the board. Other students will guess what you will buy from that department.

(Example: "Will you buy some blue jeans?" "No, I won't.")

1 **Say It** Practice the conversation with a partner.

pretty

A: Where are you going?

B: I'm going to the <u>jewelry department</u>.

A: What are you going to buy?

B: I'm not sure. I might buy <u>earrings</u> or I might buy <u>a bracelet</u>. What do you think?

A: I think you should buy the <u>earrings</u>. The <u>earrings</u> are <u>prettier</u> than the <u>bracelets</u>.

Practice the conversation again. Use the photographs below.

1. interesting

2. popular

3. romantic

GRAMMAR CHECK

might / may / will

Use *might* or *may* for future possibility.
I **might** go to the library or I **may** go home. (<u>Both</u> are possible.)

Use *will* for future certainty.
The class **will** begin at 8:00. (This is definite.)

2 **Write** Write sentences about possibilities with *might* or *may*.

1. She's going on vacation in December. <u>She might go to Florida</u>
   <u>or she may go to Las Vegas</u>   .

2. She's going to cook something delicious for dinner. _____
   _____ .

3. They're going to rent a movie tonight. _____
   _____ .

4. They're going to a good restaurant tonight. _____
   _____ .

5. He's going to buy a new book tomorrow. _____
   _____ .

Contractions with *will*

I will	=	I'll		we will	=	we'll
you will	=	you'll		they will	=	they'll
he will	=	he'll				
she will	=	she'll				
it will	=	it'll				

Check Point:

✓ With pronouns + will, it is more common to use the contraction form of *will* than the complete form.
I'**ll** see you tomorrow. (*Not:* I *will* see you tomorrow.)

Note: *Probably*

It is common to use *probably* with *will* when a future action is **likely** but isn't **certain**:
Use *probably* between *will* and the main verb. (He'll *probably* come to class.)
Use *probably* before the negative. (He probably won't come to class tomorrow.)

3 Write Answer the questions. Use a contraction and *probably* in your answers.

1. When will Arnold be back? (soon)

   <u>He'll probably be back soon</u>   .

2. When will Jennifer get a job? (next summer)

   _____ .

3. When will you go to the supermarket? (tomorrow)

   _____ .

4. What will Jack buy Jill for her birthday? (a card)

   _____ .

5. What will Lucy get from the men's department? (a shirt for her husband)

   _____ .

6. What will Rosa buy from sporting goods? (not a skateboard)

   _____ .

7. When will Cindy and Alberto get married? (not this year)

   _____ .

8. When will Davinder visit her mother-in-law? (not very soon)

   _____ .

4 **Listen** Listen and check your answers to Activity 3. Then practice the questions and answers with a partner.

> **Note: Comparative and superlative**
> Use the comparative form to compare two people or things.
> Her sofa is **more comfortable** than her chair.
> Use the superlative form to compare three or more people or things.
> Don't order **the most expensive** thing on the menu!

5 **Say It** Practice the conversation with a partner.

**delicious /
the most delicious**

A: What can I do for you?

B: I want a really <u>delicious cake</u>.

A: Then you'll probably want this one. This is <u>the most delicious cake</u> we have.

B: OK. I'll take it.

Practice the conversation again. Use the photographs below.

1. **reliable / the most reliable**

2. **large / the largest**

3. **cheap / the cheapest**

GRAMMAR CHECK

Comparative/superlative

Fill in the missing forms on the grammar chart.

	Adjective	Comparative	Superlative
one syllable	tall	taller	the tallest
	nice	nicer	_____
	big	_____	the biggest
two syllables ending in -*y*	_____	prettier	the prettiest
	funny	_____	_____
two or more syllables	beautiful	more beautiful	_____
	amazing	_____	_____
irregular	good	_____	the best
	_____	worse	the worst
	_____	farther	the farthest

6 Group Practice Work in groups of five or six. Make four lists. For example, to complete the first list, everyone should stand up. Make a list from the tallest person to the shortest person in your group in column 1. Complete column 2 of the chart indicating the people dressed in darkest to lightest clothing. Continue with columns 3 and 4 in a similar manner.

1. Tall	2. Dark clothes	3. Woke up early	4. Lives close to school
Short	Light clothes	Woke up late	Lives far from school

7 Write Look at your completed chart. Then, on a separate piece of paper, write eight superlative sentences about the people in your group. Include a few negatives.

Example: Jose isn't the **tallest** person in our group. He's the **shortest**.

8 Teamwork Task Work in teams of three or four. Write sentences about your neighborhoods using the superlative. Share your sentences with the class.

1. (cheap supermarket)   The cheap**est** supermarket in my neighborhood is _____ .
2. (big department store) _____ .
3. (delicious bakery) _____ .
4. (good restaurant) _____ .
5. (bad restaurant) _____ .
6. (interesting place to see) _____ .
7. (pretty park) _____ .

Customer Service

1 Read

Hi Jessica,

Thanks for writing to me again. Your new job sounds interesting. I'm working now as a customer service representative at a big department store.

The hours are good and the location is great. I used to work in sales. I started out in the housewares department. That's the most boring department in this store. I think that customer service is a better job than sales. I want to be the store manager one day. That's the highest position in the store. The only higher positions are executive positions in corporate headquarters in New Jersey. If you want to be a manager, you need to work in customer service, and then you have to get a promotion to an assistant sales manager position. I'm hoping to become an assistant manager in the electronics department. That's the most interesting department in the store. And if business is really slow, you can watch TV. In fact, you can watch about a hundred TVs at the same time!

Take care. Write again soon.

Your friend,
James

2 Write   Read the sentences. Circle True or False.

1. James is an assistant manager.   True   False
2. James loves his job.   True   False
3. James works in sales.   True   False
4. The housewares department is really boring.   True   False
5. James likes his work schedule.   True   False
6. James wants to work in the electronics
   department for his next job.   True   False
7. The store manager is the highest job in the store.   True   False

CRITICAL THINKING:

8. What department would you like to work in? Why?

Word Help: What's wrong with it?

There's a button missing.

There's a stain on it.

The zipper is broken.

The heel is loose.

It doesn't work.

It doesn't fit.

3 **Match** Match the sentences in Column A with the sentences in Column B.

A

1. It's the wrong size. _____
2. I can't close it. _____
3. I can't turn it on. _____
4. It looks ugly. _____
5. I can't walk in them. _____

B

a. The zipper is broken.
b. There's a stain on the sleeve.
c. It doesn't fit.
d. The heels are loose.
e. It doesn't work.

4 **Say It** Practice the conversation with a partner.

A: I'd like to return <u>this computer toy</u>.

B: Is there something wrong with <u>it</u>?

A: Yes. <u>It doesn't work</u>. <u>I can't turn it on</u>.

B: Did you buy <u>it</u> on sale?

A: Yes, I did.

B: Then I can't give you a refund. Would you like to exchange <u>it</u> for a new one? Or would you like store credit to buy something else?

A: I'll take the store credit, please.

Note: A *refund* means you get your money back.
Exchange means you change it for another one.
Store credit means you get credit to buy something else in the store.

Practice the conversation again. Use the pictures below.

1

2

3

5 **Write** Look at the advertisements below. Answer the questions about the TVs.

1. Which TV is the largest? _____ .

2. Which one is the smallest? _____ .

3. Which one is the cheapest? _____ .

4. Which one is the most expensive? _____ .

5. Which one has the longest warranty? _____ .

6. Which one has the best picture? _____ .

7. Which one is the lightest weight? _____ .

8. Which one has the biggest discount? _____ .

9. How much will you save on the Monroe today? _____ .

CRITICAL THINKING:

10. Which one would you buy? Why? _____ .

6 **Say It** Practice the conversation with a partner.

A: Do you have any TVs on sale?

B: Yes, we do. What size TV are you looking for?

A: I'd like a <u>32-inch</u>.

B: We have a <u>Stony high definition</u> TV that's on sale.

A: How much is the discount?

B: It's <u>10%</u> off.

A: And how much is the sale price?

B: The regular price is <u>$900</u>. But today's sale price is <u>$810</u>. Would you like to see it?

A: <u>That's too expensive</u>. Do you have any other TVs on sale?

B: Yes. We also have a <u>Quark TV</u>. The regular price is <u>$100</u>. Today's sale price is <u>$90</u>. Would you like to see it?

A: Yes, I would.

Practice the conversation again. Use the ads in Activity 5.

7 **Listen** Listen to the radio commercials. Write in the missing information on the ads below.

8 **Pair Practice** Work with a partner. Ask and answer the questions about the ads.

1. What is the usual cost of the cordless telephone? _____

2. How long is the 4th of July sale? _____

3. How much is the 4th of July discount? _____

4. How much do you save from the regular price if you buy it today? _____

5. How much are the sports shoes reduced this week? _____

6. What is the original price of the Pike shoe? _____

7. How much will you pay this week? _____

8. How much will you pay next week? _____

Downtown Market STORE CREDIT APPLICATION

Personal Information

1. Name
2. Phone number
3. Home address
4. City   State   Zip
5. How long at address   6. Date of birth
7. Own or rent your home
8. Name of reference
9. Relationship
10. Phone number

Employment Information

11. Employer
12. Occupation
13. Business address
14. Phone number
15. Length of present employment   16. Monthly salary

Financial References

17. Name of bank
18. Account type
19. What credit cards do you have   Amount owed

20. Signature

---

9 **Write** On which line would you write:

1. Your phone number? _____

2. The name of your bank? _____

3. That you own your home? _____

4. That you make $3,000 a month? _____

5. The name of your reference? _____

6. Your employer's name? _____

7. The name of your job? _____

8. That you have a Visa and a Discover Card? _____

10 **Write** Fill out the credit application with your information. If you don't have all the information, write as much as you can.

Homework

Cut out an advertisement from a local newspaper. Circle the important information. Bring the ad to class and tell your classmates about the product. What is it? How much does it cost? Is it on sale? How much is the discount?

Review

1 Read and Listen Read the story. Then listen to the story.

Shopping Day

Jessica and her family went shopping today at Downtown Department Store. Jessica bought the prettiest blouse she could find for her cousin Dulce. Her birthday is next week. Martin bought the coolest surfboard. It wasn't the most expensive surfboard, but it wasn't the cheapest either. Uncle Roberto bought three of the most interesting CDs he could find. Jessica's aunt tried on some perfume. Then she went to the jewelry department and saw some pretty silver earrings with purple stones. She liked them better, so she bought them instead.

Jessica bought a box of the most delicious Belgian chocolates for her teacher. She also bought some very nice things for a couple of her classmates and for a couple of her coworkers who are having a New Year's Eve party. She knows that this New Year's Eve won't be the best one of her life because she is homesick. She misses her friends and family in Colombia a lot. But she has a lot of people in Los Angeles she cares about too, so it won't be the worst New Year's Eve of her life either.

2 Write Circle the superlative adjectives in the story. Write them below. Then write the comparative and simple forms of the adjectives too.

ADJECTIVE	COMPARATIVE	SUPERLATIVE
pretty	prettier	prettiest
_____	_____	_____
_____	_____	_____
_____	_____	_____
_____	_____	_____
_____	_____	_____
_____	_____	_____

3 Listen Listen and repeat the three forms of the adjectives from the story.

4 Write Write about a gift you gave to someone in the past, or a gift that someone gave to you. What was the gift? When did you get (or give) it? Why did you get it? Where did you get it? Was it inexpensive or expensive? Was it pretty? Useful? Describe it. Use as many adjectives as you can.

5 **Best Answer** Bubble the correct answers.

a b c

1. You can find footballs in the _____ department.

   a) appliance   b) furniture   c) sporting goods   ○ ○ ○

2. She doesn't like sweets, so _____ buy her chocolates for her next birthday.

   a) I don't   b) I won't   c) I'm not   ○ ○ ○

3. The pair of silver earrings were the _____ ones in the store.

   a) prettiest   b) prettier   c) very pretty   ○ ○ ○

4. Where are you going? Don't worry, _____ be back in a few minutes.

   a) I'm   b) I'll   c) I   ○ ○ ○

5. Are you going to buy a new pair of jeans?
   I'm not sure. _____ get a pair from Grants.

   a) I might   b) I will   c) I'll   ○ ○ ○

6 **Write** Write the names of the departments in the pictures below.

1. _____

2. _____

3. _____

4. _____

5. _____

6. _____

7 **Write** Complete the dialogue with "On Sale" items from Activity 6.

A: May I help you?

B: Yes, thank you. I'm looking for a really _____ _____.

A: OK. We have a sale on _____ _____ today. How about this one?

B: Is that the _____ you have?

A: Yes, I'm afraid it is.

B: OK. Thank you anyway.

8 **Group Practice** Work in groups of five or six. Choose one student to play the salesperson. Other students choose one item from Activity 6 that they are looking for. Each student should choose a different item. Tell the salesperson what you are looking for. Use the dialogue from Activity 7.

9 **Teamwork Task** Work in teams of 4 or 5. Work together to write superlative sentences about your classmates. Follow the example.

1. (young) _The youngest person in our class is_ _____ .
2. (tall) _____ .
3. (short) _____ .
4. (funny) _____ .
5. (quiet) _____ .
6. (talkative) _____ .
7. (friendly) _____ .
8. (serious) _____ .
9. (old) _____ .
10. (studious) _____ .

Pronunciation The /b/ sound vs. the /v/ sound
The *b* sound is made with the two lips. The *v* sound is made with teeth and the bottom lip.

A. Practice making these two sounds.

B. Listen and repeat. Notice the difference between the *b* sound and the *v* sound.

boat vote	berry very	bow vow	base vase
best vest	ban van	bet vet	curb curve

C. Now listen to pairs of words. If they are the same, write *S*. If they are different, write *D*.

1. _____   3. _____   5. _____   7. _____   9 _____
2. _____   4. _____   6. _____   8. _____   10. _____

INTERNET IDEA
Shopping Online
Choose one item you want to buy, such as a jacket, a pair of blue jeans, or a book. Try to find three different Internet sites where you can buy the item. Compare the prices. Report to the class.

I can…			
• identify sections of a department store.	1	2	3
• ask for and give locations.	1	2	3
• interpret a bar graph.	1	2	3
• make predictions using *will* or *won't*.	1	2	3
• talk about future possibilities.	1	2	3
• rank people and things using superlative adjectives.	1	2	3
• describe product defects.	1	2	3
• return or exchange an item.	1	2	3
• understand advertisements.	1	2	3
• compare ads.	1	2	3
• fill out a credit application.	1	2	3

1 = not well   2 = OK   3 = very well

DOWNTOWN

10 **Write** Write the missing words in the cartoon story. Use these words: *she'll, women's, entertainment, cosmetics, jewelry, prettiest, cutest, best, most, won't.*

Alberto: The (1)_____ important thing is to find the right birthday gift for Cindy.
David: There's the (2)_____ department. How about some really nice perfume?

Alberto: She (3)_____ be happy with perfume. She doesn't wear it very much.
David: There's the (4)_____ section. How about some interesting CDs?

Alberto: That's too cheap. I have to get her something more expensive than that.
David: There's the (5)_____ department. You can get her a diamond ring.
Alberto: Not *that* expensive! That's too serious!

David: There's the (6)_____ department. You can get her a cute blouse or a pretty jacket.
Alberto: She already has the (7)_____ blouses and the (8)_____ jackets in the world.

David: You know, she already has the (9)_____ gift you can give.
Alberto: What do you mean?
David: You give her your time. You see her every day! Isn't that the best gift two people can give each other?

Alberto: Hmmm, maybe it is.
Alberto: But I think (10)_____ still want something else, too!
David: Yeah, I guess you're right.

11 **Pair Practice** Practice the cartoon story with a partner.

Health and Safety

1 **Read and Listen** *Read the story. Look at the picture. Then listen to the story. Then match the numbers in the picture to the words in the box.*

Emergency!

Alex had a terrible day yesterday. He was in a car accident on his way to work. He had to call 911 to report the emergency. A woman didn't see a "One Way" street sign and crashed into his car. Unfortunately, Alex wasn't wearing his seat belt so he hit his head on the windshield and cut his forehead. After a few minutes, two Emergency Medical Technicians arrived. They put the woman on a stretcher and took her blood pressure, pulse, and temperature. Then they put her in the ambulance and took her to the hospital. They took Alex to the hospital, too. "You might have a concussion," they said. The woman didn't obey a safety sign and Alex didn't obey a safety rule so now they were both going to the hospital.

crash = bump or knock into very hard
concussion = a serious head injury
emergency = an event needing immediate help

_____ temperature
_____ ambulance
_____ emergency
_____ blood pressure
_____ cut
_____ emergency medical technician
_____ pulse
_____ stretcher
_____ safety rule
_____ safety sign
_____ neck brace

What's the Problem?

> **Safety Tip: Dial 911**
> When there is an emergency, dial 911. Explain the emergency in simple, clear words. Give the location of the emergency. Be as specific as possible.

1 **Say It** Practice the conversation with a partner.

son / wrist

A: Dr. Casey's office.

B: I'd like to make an appointment to see the doctor.

A: OK. What's the problem?

B: My <u>son</u> hurt <u>his wrist</u>. <u>He's</u> in a lot of pain. I think it might be broken.

A: Can you bring <u>him</u> in at 3:00?

B: Yes. We'll be there at 3:00.

appointment	in pain	broken

Practice the conversation again. Use the pictures below.

1. daughter / elbow

2. husband / ankle

3. grandmother / hip

2 **Pair Practice** Work with a partner. What else might be broken? Make a list of other body parts that might be broken. Then practice more conversations with your partner.

leg_____ _____ _____ _____

_____ _____ _____ _____

3 Match Match the problems with the body parts. Then write a sentence using the new phrase.

1. a black _____   **a.** tooth   _____ .

2. a pain in someone's _____   **b.** ankle   _____ .

3. a sprained _____   **c.** eye   _____ .

4. a sore _____   **d.** throat   _____ .

5. a bloody _____   **e.** shoulders   _____ .

6. sunburned _____   **f.** nose   _____ .

4 Write Write the words below in the correct places in the pictures.

ankle	thigh	neck	nose	shoulders	stomach
back	chest	eye	waist	arm	hand
foot	toes	hips	heel	ear	earlobe
fingers	chin	lips	teeth	calf	
mouth	eyebrow	eyelid	forehead		
leg	elbow	wrist	knee		

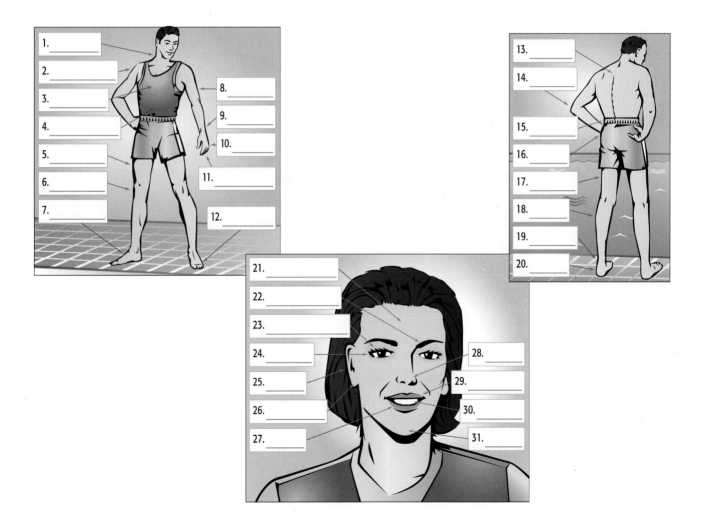

1. _____
2. _____
3. _____
4. _____
5. _____
6. _____
7. _____
8. _____
9. _____
10. _____
11. _____
12. _____
13. _____
14. _____
15. _____
16. _____
17. _____
18. _____
19. _____
20. _____
21. _____
22. _____
23. _____
24. _____
25. _____
26. _____
27. _____
28. _____
29. _____
30. _____
31. _____

5 **Listen** Listen and check your answers to Activity 4 on page 145. Then listen again and repeat for pronunciation.

6 **Write** Complete the sentences with the correct body part from Activity 4.

1. I wear my belt around my _____ .

2. There are ten _____ on my feet.

3. My _____ connects my head and shoulders.

4. My _____ is between my calf and thigh.

5. My _____ is above my eyebrows.

6. My _____ is at the back of my foot.

7. My _____ is at the bottom of my face.

8. My _____ are the doors on my eyes.

7 **Say It** Practice the conversation with a partner.

A: What do you do when you have a <u>headache</u>?

B: When I have a <u>headache</u>, I <u>take aspirin</u>. What do you do?

A: When I have a <u>headache</u>, I usually <u>take ibuprofen</u>.

**headache /
take aspirin**

Practice the conversation again. Use the photographs below and your own information.

**1. sore throat /
drink tea with honey**

**2. cold /
take cold medicine**

**3. backache /
rest and take aspirin**

Culture Tip

Emergency Rooms

Hospital emergency rooms are for emergencies only. Don't go to a hospital for minor problems like a cold or a sore throat. What should you go to the emergency room for?

8 **Group Practice** Find out how healthy you and your classmates are! Interview two of your classmates. Use the chart below. Ask "Do you . . .?" questions. Write the number of points under his or her name if a students says "Yes" to a question. For example, if he sleeps seven to eight hours a night, write two points under his name. The student with the most points has the healthiest lifestyle. Who has the healthiest lifestyle in your class?

	NAME	NAME	YOUR NAME
A. SHOULD			
1. Sleep seven to eight hours a night (2 points)			
2. Exercise for thirty minutes three times a week (2 points)			
3. Eat a lot of fruit (1 point)			
4. Eat vegetables every day (1 point)			
5. Go to the doctor every year (1 point)			
6. Eat fish at least twice a week (1 point)			
7. Get together with friends at least once a week (1 point)			
8. Do something that makes you laugh frequently (1 point)			
9. Have a job you like (2 points)			
Add the points. Points:			
B. SHOULDN'T			
10. Eat a lot of sugar (1 point)			
11. Sleep less than 6 hours a day (1 point)			
12. Eat at fast food restaurants almost every day (2 points)			
13. Smoke cigarettes every day (3 points)			
14. Drink a lot of alcohol (2 points)			
15. Drink a lot of coffee (1 point)			
16. Watch TV more than three hours a day (1 point)			
Now add these points. Points:			
Subtract these points from the points above.			
Write the totals. Total:			

Who has the healthiest lifestyle in your class? _____

Game Time

Teacher Says

Stand up. Listen to your teacher. If you hear "Teacher says touch your elbow," you should touch your elbow. If you hear only "Touch your elbow," don't touch your elbow. If you make a mistake, sit down.

Safety Rules

1 **Say It** Practice the conversation with a partner.

A: Look at the sign.

B: What does it mean?

A: It means you must <u>not smoke</u> here.

B: I'm sorry. What does it mean?

A: It means "<u>No Smoking</u>".

B: Oh. I understand.

smoke

Practice the conversation again. Use the pictures below.

stop   run   enter   park

GRAMMAR CHECK

Must / must not and *have to / not have to*		
	Definition	**Example**
must = have to	something is necessary or required	You **must** pass a driving test to get a driver's license. You **have to** pass a driving test to get a driver's license.
must not	something that is not permitted	You **must not** drive through a red light.

Check Point:

✓ *Must not* and *not have to* have different meanings:

—*not have to* = isn't necessary, or is optional.

—*must not* = something that is not permitted

You **don't have to** wait for me, but you can if you wish. (It's your choice)

You **must not** smoke in the classroom.

2 **Write** Complete the sentences with *must, must not,* or *don't have to.*

1. Employees _____ be late for work.

2. Students _____ park in staff parking spaces.

3. Students _____ bring their lunch to school.

4. In our class, students _____ do homework.

5. In our class, students _____ come to class every day.

6. Students _____ eat food during class.

1

DO NOT PASS

2

NOTICE
WASH HANDS BEFORE LEAVING RESTROOM

3

WE NEED YOU
BUCKLE UP

4

NO SWIMMING

5

SPEED LIMIT 65
MINIMUM 45

6

3 **Write** Write a *must* or *must not* sentence for each of the signs.

1. _____ .

2. _____ .

3. _____ .

4. _____ .

5. _____ .

6. _____ .

4 **Group Practice** Work in groups of three or four. Work together to write some personal and home safety rules. Write as many as you can.

Example: Children must not talk to strangers.
     You must lock your doors when you go to bed at night.

Read your list to the class. Ask if they agree or disagree with your rules.

_____

_____

_____

_____

_____

_____

5 **Say It** Practice the conversation with a partner.

have an accident

A: Watch out!

B: What's the matter?

A: <u>Don't turn right</u>.

B: Why?

A: If you <u>turn right</u>, you might <u>have an accident</u>.

B: Oh, thanks. I didn't see the sign.

A: You're welcome.

Practice the conversation again. Use the pictures below.

1. get an expensive ticket

2. get a speeding ticket

3. slip and fall

6 **Group Practice** Work in groups of three or four. Work together to complete the sentences below with interesting conclusions.

1. If you eat too much sweet food, you might _____ .

2. If you don't sleep enough at night, _____ .

3. If you drink too much coffee, _____ .

4. If you study English every day, _____ .

5. If you cross the street without looking both ways, _____

_____ .

6. If José lifts that heavy box without bending his knees, _____

_____ .

7 **Listen** Listen to the interview with Alex about his car accident. Fill in the missing information on the form.

Employee Accident Report
- please print clearly -

To be completed by employee

NAME: Alex Marenko   EMPLOYEE NUMBER: 605008

DATE OF ACCIDENT: _____   TIME: _____

LOCATION: Beach St. and Ocean Ave, Santa Monica, California

NATURE OF INJURIES
BODY PART: forehead _____ WHAT KIND OF INJURY: _____ bruises

DID ACCIDENT OCCUR WHILE AT WORK OR WHILE PERFORMING JOB DUTIES? ☑ YES   ☐ NO

WERE OTHER PEOPLE INVOLVED?   ☑ YES   ☐ NO

IF YES, WHO ELSE WAS INVOLVED? The driver of the other car

DESCRIBE IN YOUR OWN WORDS WHAT HAPPENED: It was a _____.

I was _____ on Beach Street when a woman turned

_____ on a _____ and hit me.

My head hit the windshield and I _____.

I also _____.

SIGNATURE: *Alex Marenko*   DATE: 9/21/05

---

8 **Write** Answer the questions about Alex's accident.

1. How many people were involved in the accident? _____ .

2. When did the accident occur? _____ .

3. Was Alex working when he had the accident? _____ .

4. Who was hurt? _____ .

5. What parts of his body did Alex hurt? _____ .

9 **Teamwork Task** Work in teams of three or four. Make a list of class rules for your class.

IN OUR CLASS STUDENTS . . .

MUST	MUST NOT	DON'T HAVE TO
_____	_____	_____
_____	_____	_____
_____	_____	_____
_____	_____	_____

Emergencies

1 **Read**

Hi Jessica.

Thanks for writing. You asked me about my job, so I'll tell you a little about it. My job title is Emergency Medical Technician, also called an EMT. Some people call us paramedics. It's a little like being a doctor, but you don't have to go to medical school. Of course you don't make the kind of money doctors make either.

It is a stressful job. While you are working, you must be ready for a terrible emergency at any moment. I'll give you an example. Last night while we were driving back to the garage, we got a call about a serious car accident. Three people were very badly hurt. One of them was a six-year-old girl. She was bleeding a lot and was already in shock when we arrived. I stopped the bleeding and got her into the ambulance and drove her to the hospital very quickly. I probably saved her life!

In some ways my job isn't a very good job. For example, the pay isn't very high. But in other ways it is a great job. It's nice to know that I am helping people who really need me. People don't have to say "thank you." Sometimes in the ambulance they just hold my hand and I can see the "thank you" in their eyes. At those times I feel like I have a very important job.

Your friend,

Laura

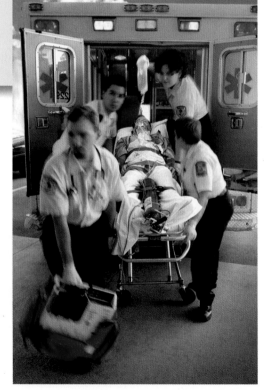

2 Write

1. Why is Laura's job stressful? _____.

2. What was the emergency Laura went to last night? _____.

3. How was the little girl when Laura arrived? _____.

4. What did Laura do for the little girl when she arrived? _____.

5. What does Laura like about her job? _____.

CRITICAL THINKING:

6. Does Laura have a good job? Why or why not? _____

_____.

3 Say It Practice the conversation with a partner.

had an accident / getting on the freeway

A: This is Mario. I'm going to be late for work today.

B: Why? What happened?

A: I <u>had an accident</u> while I was <u>getting on the freeway</u>.

B: Oh, I'm sorry to hear that. Are you okay?

A: Yes, I think so. I should be at work in a couple of hours.

B: OK. I'll let the supervisor know. Thank you for calling.

Practice the conversations again. Use the pictures below.

1. **got bit by a dog /
   walking to my car**

2. **slipped and fell /
   taking a shower**

3. **hurt my back /
   playing tennis**

GRAMMAR CHECK

Past continuous		
Subject	**Past Continuous**	
I/He, She	**was exercising**	at 8:00 last night.
It	**was snowing**	a lot, so we drove slowly.
We/You/They	**were eating**	when the telephone rang.

Check Point:

✓ Use past continuous to talk about a continuing action at a specific time in the past.

✓ Use past continuous with *while*. while = at the same time

She came home **while** he was cooking dinner.

4 **Write** Write true answers to the questions.

1. What were you doing at 8:00 this morning? _____ .

2. What were you doing yesterday at 11:30 A.M.? _____ .

3. What were you doing yesterday at 4:00 P.M.? _____ .

4. What were you doing yesterday evening at 6:00? _____ .

5. What were you doing last night at 9:30? _____ .

5 **Pair Practice** Ask and answer the questions in Activity 4. Then ask about other times of day.

6 **Write** Complete the sentences with *while* clauses.

1. She fell and hurt her back while _____ .

2. He met his wife while _____ .

3. They got lost while _____ .

4. I found some money while _____ .

5. He lost his keys while _____ .

7 **Group Practice** Work in groups of five or six. Student 1: Tell the teacher what you were doing last night at 8:00. Student 2: Tell the teacher what you were doing while Student 1 was . . .-*ing*. Student 3: Tell the teacher what you were doing at the same time. Use *while*.

Example: "I was cooking dinner while José was taking a shower and Rosa was working."

Continue until the last student tells what all the other students were doing.

Employee Medical History Form	To be completed by employee

- please print clearly -

1. NAME: _____ EMPLOYEE #: _____

2. ADDRESS: _____ TELEPHONE #: _____

3. ARE YOU CURRENTLY SEEING A DOCTOR FOR ANY MEDICAL PROBLEM? ☐ YES ☐ NO

IF YES, EXPLAIN: _____

4. ARE YOU CURRENTLY TAKING ANY MEDICATION? ☐ YES ☐ NO

IF YES, EXPLAIN: _____

5. HAVE YOU EVER HAD MAJOR SURGERY? ☐ YES ☐ NO

IF YES, EXPLAIN: _____

6. WHAT OTHER MEDICAL PROBLEMS HAVE YOU HAD? List below.

_____

7. DO YOU HAVE ANY PROBLEMS OR CONDITIONS THAT MIGHT AFFECT YOUR ABILITY TO WORK? ☐ YES ☐ NO

IF YES, EXPLAIN: _____

8. SIGNATURE: _____ DATE: _____

8 **Write** On what line of the medical history form, if any, should Mr. Chung explain the following:

1. The medicine he takes regularly for headaches. _____

2. The hip operation he had for arthritis. _____

3. The regular checkups he gets for his arthritis. _____

4. The pneumonia he had three years ago. _____

5. The fact that he can't stand up for very long because of his arthritis. _____

6. The cold he had last month. _____

7. Where should he sign his name? _____

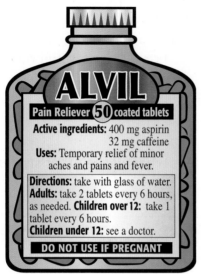
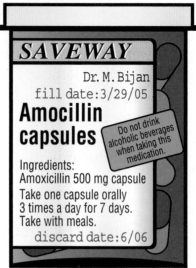

9 Pair Practice Work with a partner. Look at the medicine labels. Ask and answer the questions. Then ask more questions about the medicine.

1. Which one is an "over-the-counter" medicine? _____

2. Which one requires a prescription? _____

3. Who prescribed it? _____

4. How often should you take Amocillin? _____

5. How many capsules should you take? _____

6. How should you take the Alvil? _____

7. How should you take the Amocillin? _____

8. What are the warnings each of the medicines have? _____

_____

10 Teamwork Task

CRITICAL THINKING: CONTRAST AND COMPARE

Work in teams of three or four. Compare the two medications. How are they different? Work together to write sentences below. Use *must, must not,* or *don't have to* as much as possible. Write as many sentences as you can.

Example:

You must have a prescription for Amocillin, but you don't have to have . . .

_____

_____

_____

_____

_____

_____

1 Read and Listen Read the story. Then listen to the story.

The Earthquake

When Jessica thinks about emergencies, she usually thinks about the earthquake she experienced when she was in high school. She was sitting in her classroom when she heard a loud crack and the whole classroom started to shake violently. Her friend, Maura, was writing on the blackboard when the earthquake hit. She dropped the chalk and screamed. While the room was shaking, Jessica put her head under her desk. One of her classmates—Oscar—got up and tried to run out of the room. He fell and broke his arm.

The earthquake experience taught Jessica a few things. She learned that you shouldn't try to run during an earthquake. You must get down under something strong and cover your head. And you must not panic! Panic puts everybody in more danger. She also learned that you should have a flashlight and bottled water at home. And she learned that you must have a first-aid kit just in case somebody does get hurt.

2 Write Answer the questions with complete sentences.

1. What was Jessica doing when the earthquake hit?

   _____ .

2. What was Maura doing when the earthquake hit?

   _____ .

3. What did Oscar do wrong while the room was shaking?

   _____ .

4. What happened to Oscar?

   _____ .

5. What mustn't you do during an emergency?

   _____ .

6. What must you have at home? Why?

   _____ .

CRITICAL THINKING:

7. What are some other things you should do to prepare for an emergency?

   _____ .

3 **Write** On a separate piece of paper, write about an emergency you saw or experienced. Where were you? What were people doing before the emergency? What happened? Was anybody hurt? What were you doing before the emergency started? What did you do during and after the emergency?

4 **Best Answer** Bubble the correct answers.   **a**   **b**   **c**

1. The phone rang while I was _____ dinner.

    a) eat   **b)** eating   **c)** ate   ◯   ◯   ◯

2. You _____ have a driver's license if you want to drive a car.

    a) should   **b)** must   **c)** need   ◯   ◯   ◯

3. If you _____ too fast, you might get a speeding ticket.

    a) will drive   **b)** driving   **c)** drive   ◯   ◯   ◯

4. What was she doing at 8:00? She _____.

    a) was working   **b)** worked   **c)** is working   ◯   ◯   ◯

5. He hurt his whole leg, but the worst damage was to the _____.

    a) wrist   **b)** ankle   **c)** elbow   ◯   ◯   ◯

5 **Write** Complete the conversation. You are calling your boss's secretary. Tell her you are going to be late for work because you were involved in an accident. Tell her about the accident. Tell her what time you will be in.

    A: Acme Business Supplies. This is Tina.

    B: Hello, Tina. This is _____.

    A: What can I do for you, _____.

    B: I'm afraid _____.

    A: Why? What happened?

    B: _____.

    A: Oh, I'm sorry to hear that. Are you okay?

    B: _____.

6 **Pair Practice** Practice the conversation in Activity 5 with a partner.

___

___

___

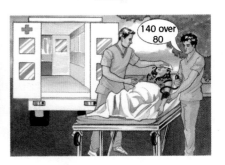

___

___

___

___

___

___

8 **Write** Look at the pictures. On a separate piece of paper, write the story of Rosa's car accident. Write as many sentences as you can. Remember to use past continuous and simple past in your story.

9 **Teamwork Task** Work in teams of three or four. Work together to create a list of rules for a family. Use *must, must not,* and *not have to.* You can make funny rules or serious ones. You can makes rules for the husband, the wife, the teenage kids, or kids of any other age. You can even make rules for the uncle or the mother-in-law.

Example: "The wife or husband doesn't have to cook dinner every night. The family must eat dinner together twice a week."

Example: "The teenage kids must . . ."

Write as many rules as you can.

Pronunciation Silent letters

Many words in English have silent letters. These are letters you see on paper but don't pronounce. Listen and repeat the words below.

knee   wrist   calf   elbow   neck   waist   back   thigh

Now cross out the silent letters in each word. Check your answers with a partner.

INTERNET IDEA
Driving Safety
Learn more about basic traffic signs, safety, and signals by going to the Web site for the Department of Motor Vehicles in your state. Share your findings with a partner, small group, or your class.

I can . . .			
• describe medical problems.	1	2	3
• identify parts of the face and body.	1	2	3
• describe medical treatments.	1	2	3
• talk about healthy and unhealthy behavior.	1	2	3
• understand safety rules.	1	2	3
• use must / must not and have to / not have to.	1	2	3
• use the past continuous.	1	2	3
• give and respond to safety warnings.	1	2	3
• understand an accident report.	1	2	3
• call in late for work.	1	2	3
• fill out a medical history form.	1	2	3
• compare prescription and over-the-counter medications.	1	2	3

1 = not well   2 = OK   3 = very well

Alberto: There was a bad (1)_____ today in the warehouse.
Cindy: Really? What happened?

Alberto: Jackson (2)_____ a forklift while he (3)_____ music on his headphones.

Cindy: That's terrible! I guess Jackson didn't obey the (4)_____.

Alberto: That's right. He wasn't paying attention to his job. That's a safety rule on every job. As a result, he (5)_____ into a stack of boxes and they fell over onto the warehouse manager.

Alberto: We had to call 911. The EMTs came in an (6)_____ and took the manager's (7)_____ and all that.
Cindy: How is he?
Alberto: He's okay. He just has some (8)_____ on his back and forehead.

Cindy: What happened to Jackson?
Alberto: He's OK, but he (9)_____ pay for the damaged boxes.
Cindy: I'm sure everyone learned an important lesson.
Alberto: They certainly did!

11 Pair Practice Practice the cartoon story with a partner.

On the Job

GOALS

- ✓ Ask for and offer help
- ✓ Accept and decline help
- ✓ Describe steps in a process
- ✓ Request a schedule change
- ✓ Use object, reflexive, and possessive pronouns
- ✓ Use phrasal verbs
- ✓ Use *because* and *so*
- ✓ Use *someone*, *anyone*, *everyone*, and *no one*
- ✓ Read an employee evaluation form
- ✓ Give and respond to criticism
- ✓ Give and take telephone messages
- ✓ Make and respond to requests
- ✓ Read a paycheck stub

① Read and Listen *Read the story. Look at the pictures. Listen to the story. Then write what each worker is doing.*

Many people work at the Downtown Supermarket. Cindy works in the bakery department. She makes and serves coffee and pastries to customers, too. Ralph is the store butcher. He cuts and wraps the meat and sometimes helps customers decide what kind of meat to buy. He knows a lot about different kinds of meat. Tomás works in the office. He is the store manager. He hires and **fires** workers and completes the employee evaluations. Tomás fills out an employee evaluation form for each employee once a year. Rosa works in the office. Her title is Office Assistant. She makes the weekly work schedule and reports the hours for all the employees. Lupe is a cashier. She takes money from the customers and gives them **change**. Timmy helps her at the checkout stand. He bags the groceries when the store is busy. He **stocks** the shelves, too.

fire = opposite of *hire*
change = extra money given back after buying something
stock = fill, put more groceries on

WHAT ARE THEY DOING NOW?

1. <u>Cindy is serving coffee and a pastry to a customer.</u>

2. _____

3. _____

4. _____

5. _____

6. _____

Need Any Help?

1 **Say It** Practice the conversation with a partner.

A: Does anybody need any help?

B: Yes. <u>This box is really heavy</u>. I can't <u>carry</u> it. Can you help me, please?

A: No problem. I'll <u>carry it</u> for you.

B: Thanks. I appreciate it.

carry

Practice the conversation again. Use the pictures below.

> **Note:** Use *will* for offers to help
>
> **Example:** Bill **will** help you move that box now, or I**'ll** help you later!

1. solve   2. open   3. catch

Talk about other things you can't do. Your partner will offer to help.

GRAMMAR CHECK

Object pronouns after prepositions

Use object pronouns (*me, you, him, her, it, us, them*) after prepositions.
She bought flowers **for him**.
You can count **on me**.

2 **Write** Rewrite the sentences using object pronouns after the prepositions.

1. Please don't complain about Mr. Davis. _____

2. He fixed the sink for Mrs. King. _____

3. Is she giving the car to Jack and Jill? _____

4. Does she live above the Simpsons? _____

5. She is planning a party for her brother. _____

6. Were you looking at Monica or at Joey? _____

Reflexive pronouns

Singular	Plural
myself	ourselves
yourself	yourselves
himself / herself / itself	themselves

Check Point:

✓ When the subject and object are the *same*, use a reflexive pronoun, not an object pronoun.

I am looking in the mirror. **I** am looking at **myself**. (correct)

I am looking at *me*. (*not* correct)

3 **Say It** Practice the conversation with a partner.

change the tire

A: <u>Does Manuel</u> need any help?

B: No, <u>he doesn't</u>. <u>He</u> can <u>change the tire</u> by <u>himself</u>.

A: Are you sure?

B: Yes, I'm sure.

Practice the conversation again. Use the pictures below.

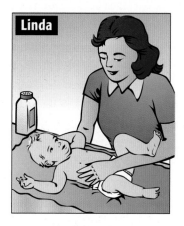
1. change the diaper

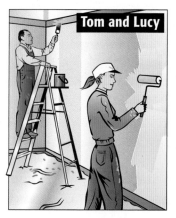
2. paint the living room

3. find the stadium

4 **Pair Practice** Ask your partner about students in your class. (*Does José need any help? No, he doesn't. He can . . . himself*). Use the ideas below or think of different activities.

read the chapter	find a job
order a pizza	make dinner
study for the test	fill out the application

5 **Say It** Practice the conversation with a partner.

A: Does anyone need help with anything?

B: Yes, <u>Cindy</u> does.

A: What does <u>she</u> need?

B: <u>She</u> doesn't know how to <u>make cappuccino</u>.

A: No problem. I'll show <u>her</u> how.

make cappuccino

Practice the conversation again. Use the pictures below.

1. fill out his time card

2. print the new evaluation forms

3. correct a credit card mistake

GRAMMAR CHECK

someone/somebody/anyone/anybody/everyone/everybody/no one/nobody

Positive Statements	**Someone** (= **Somebody**) is in the office. (At least *one* person)
	Everyone (= **Everybody**) is in the office. (*All* the people in a specific group)
Negative Statement	**No one** (= **Nobody**) is working right now.
Question	Is **anyone** (= **anybody**) working right now? Yes, **someone** is. No, **nobody** is.

6 **Pair Practice** Work with a partner. Ask and answer questions about the students in your class.

Example: Is **anyone** listening to the teacher? Yes, **everyone** is.

Use the ideas below, or use your own.

using a dictionary?	wearing a hat?	standing up?
holding a pencil?	talking to the teacher?	absent from class?

7 **Say It** Practice the conversation with a partner.

1. put the paper in face down
2. punch in the fax number
3. press START
4. pick up your fax receipt

A: Could you please show me how to use the <u>fax machine</u>?

B: Sure. I'd be happy to. First, you <u>put the paper in face down</u>.

A: OK.

B: Next, you <u>punch in the fax number</u>. Then, you <u>press START</u>.

A: <u>Punch in the number</u> and <u>press START</u>.

B: Then you <u>pick up your fax receipt</u>. <u>It tells you that the fax was received</u>. That's all there is to it.

A: Great. Thanks a lot!

Practice the conversation again. Use the pictures below.

1. put a new filter in the holder
2. add coffee to the filter
3. place the coffee pot under the filter
4. press the ON button

1. type the Web address for *Downtown English*
2. type in your password
3. click OK
4. click on the level you need

8 **Teamwork Task** Work in teams of three or four. Write step-by-step directions for things you know how to do. (Example: a recipe for something you can cook) Write as many steps as you can. Share with the class.

Game Time

Telephone

Work in a group of seven to ten students. Student 1: Write something interesting on a piece of paper. It must be at least ten words. (Example: We are going to have a difficult English grammar test on Thursday.) Don't let anybody see it. Whisper the sentence to Student 2. Student 2: Whisper the sentence to Student 3. Continue until the last student hears the sentence. Then ask him or her what he or she heard. Compare his sentence to the original sentence. If they are different, find out where the mistakes happened. Ask: What did Student 1 tell Student 2? What did Student 2 tell Student 3?, etc.

GRAMMAR CHECK ✓

Possessive pronouns

Subject pronoun	Possessive adjective	Possessive pronouns
I	my	mine
you	your	yours
he	his	his
she	her	hers
it	its	its
we	our	ours
they	their	theirs

Check Points:

✓ Use possessive adjectives **together with** a noun.
  That's **my book**.

✓ Use possessive pronouns **in place of** a noun.
  That's **mine**.

1 **Say It** Practice the conversation with a partner.

A: Please give <u>this pen</u> to <u>Mr. Garcia</u>. It's <u>his</u>.

B: OK. I'll give it to <u>him</u> right away.

A: Don't forget.

B: Don't worry. I won't.

Mr. Garcia

Practice the conversation again. Use the pictures below.

1. Maria

2. the people upstairs

3. me

4. our department

2 **Listen** Listen to the sentences and circle the words you hear.

1. **a.** her   **b.** hers

2. **a.** our   **b.** ours

3. **a.** their   **b.** theirs

4. **a.** my   **b.** mine

5. **a.** her   **b.** hers

3 **Write** Fill in the blanks with possessive adjectives, possessive pronouns, or object pronouns.

1. Please call Mrs. Park. Here's _____ phone number.

2. They have a black car. Is that black car _____?

3. We really need _____ *Newbury House Dictionary* back. Please return it to _____.

4. You have a leather jacket, don't you? Is this leather jacket _____?

5. She doesn't have an air conditioner in _____ office.

6. Ms. Lemonis has a new computer. Is that computer _____?

7. Please give me that grocery cart. It's _____.

8. They called yesterday. I'll call _____ back tomorrow.

4 **Say It** Practice the conversation with a partner.

pick up my mother at the airport

A: Mr. Lopez, may I talk to you about something?

B: Sure, Ana. What is it?

A: May I change my work schedule next week?

B: What do you want to change?

A: I want to take next Friday off because I have to <u>pick up my mother at the airport</u>.

B: That's a good reason. I'm glad you told me today. I'll get somebody to cover for you.

A: Thanks. I appreciate it.

5 **Pair Practice** Read the list of reasons below. Decide together if they are good reasons or bad reasons for taking an afternoon off from your job.

	GOOD REASON	BAD REASON
a. attend my daughter's graduation	_____	_____
b. wait for the heating company to come fix the heat	_____	_____
c. go to a baseball game	_____	_____
d. take my son to the doctor	_____	_____
e. cook dinner for some visiting relatives	_____	_____
f. attend my sister's wedding	_____	_____

Use the good reasons to practice the conversation again.

6 Say It Practice the conversation with a partner.

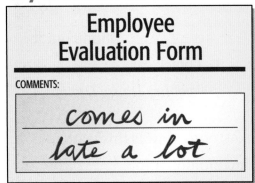

come in earlier

A: Can I talk to you about something?

B: Yes, of course, Mr. Lopez.

A: I read your evaluation form. <u>You come in late a lot</u>.

B: I'm sorry, I know it's a problem. I'll try to <u>come in earlier</u>.

A: Please try. It's important.

B: I understand. I promise I'll do my best.

Practice the conversation again. Use the comments below.

1. take shorter breaks

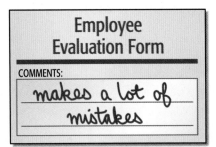

2. be more careful

3. work faster

> **Note:** Use *will* for promises. They take place in the future.
> **Example:** I **will try** to return this book to you by tomorrow.

7 Group Practice Work in groups of five. Student 1 is the supervisor. Students 2 to 5 are employees. Write the four employees' names in the boxes below. Then write appropriate promises for each of the four students. Finally, practice the conversation again like the ones in Activity 6.

NAME	COMMENT	PROMISE
	often dresses unprofessionally	
	doesn't obey safety rules	
	talks too much on the job	
	often argues with coworkers	

8 **Listen** Listen to Tomás talking to four of his employees. Complete the evaluation form below. Use these words: *Excellent, Good, Fair,* and *Poor.*

Employee Evaluation Form

Name	Attendance	Punctuality	Appearance	Work habits	Gets along with coworkers?
Betsy	Excellent		Excellent	Good	
Carla		Fair			Excellent
Timmy	Fair			Fair	Good
Luis		Excellent	Good		

9 **Write** Match Column A with Column B.

A

1. ____ good attendance
2. ____ gets along well with people
3. ____ punctual
4. ____ appearance
5. ____ good work habits

B

a. you arrive on time
b. how you look
c. you are friendly
d. you are a hard worker
e. you come to work every day

10 **Write** Look at the chart to answer the questions.

1. Who always comes to work? _____ .
2. Who is always friendly? _____ .
3. Who comes to work late a lot? _____ .
4. Who never comes to work late? _____ .
5. Who always looks good at work? _____ .
6. Who is the hardest worker? _____ .

CRITICAL THINKING:

7. Pretend all four of the workers want to work for YOUR business. You can only hire one. Which one would you hire? Why? _____ .

11 **Teamwork Task** Work in teams of four. Complete the chart below, giving examples for the categories. If someone comes to work without their hair combed, is that an example of good appearance?

	APPEARANCE	WORK HABITS	PUNCTUALITY	GETS ALONG WITH COWORKERS?
Good				
Bad				
Good				
Bad				

The Office

1 **Read** Read this e-mail from Silvia, Jessica's friend.

> Hi Jessica,
>
> Thanks for writing. So, you are interested in hearing about people's jobs in the United States. I'll tell you about mine. My job title is Office Assistant, so, of course, I work in an office. What do I do every day?
>
> Most of the day I answer telephones and take messages. But first, in the morning, I turn on my computer and check my e-mail. I have three bosses! Sometimes one of the bosses sends me an e-mail with a job for me to do. If that happens, I do that work right away. Next, I open the mail from the post office. (They call it the "snail mail.") The "junk mail"—things like advertisements—I just throw away. I put the more important mail in our staff's office mailboxes. I give my bosses' mail to them. Finally, I go to the sales office and answer telephones.
>
> Sometimes customers call with questions. I don't sell anything, but I help the salespeople. So, if you want to buy a copy machine, I'd be happy to answer any questions you have. (Just joking!)
>
> Take care, Jessica.
>
> Your friend,
> Silvia

2 **Write** Answer the questions about Silvia's e-mail.

1. What does Silvia do first thing in the morning? _____

2. What do the bosses sometimes send her? _____

3. What is "snail mail"? _____

4. What is "junk mail"? _____

5. Does Silvia throw away all the "snail mail"? _____

6. What does she do in the sales office? _____

CRITICAL THINKING:

7. Is Silvia a salesperson? Why or why not? _____

3 **Say It** Practice the conversation with a partner.

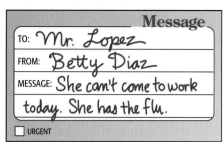

TO: Mr. Lopez
FROM: Betty Diaz
MESSAGE: She can't come to work today. She has the flu.
☐ URGENT

A: This is <u>Betsy Diaz</u>. I'm calling for <u>Mr. Lopez</u>.

B: <u>He</u> isn't in right now. Would you like to leave <u>him</u> a message?

A: Yes, please. Tell <u>him</u> I'm very sorry, but <u>I can't come in to work today because I have the flu</u>.

B: OK. I'll tell <u>him</u>.

Culture Tip

Always call as soon as possible if you can't go to work. You should also call if you are going to be late for a business appointment or meeting. You should also say you're sorry.

4 **Listen** Listen to the conversations. Complete the messages below.

Message
TO: Ms. Carter
FROM: Tania _____
MESSAGE: She is going to be _____ for the _____. She has car trouble. She _____ be there by _____.
☐ URGENT

Message
TO: Bill
FROM: MARY
MESSAGE: She is _____ but she _____ with you tonight. She has to go to a budget meeting _____.
☐ URGENT

Message
TO: Mr. Ryan
FROM: Alex Marenko
MESSAGE: He's _____ absent on _____. He has to _____.
☐ URGENT

5 **Pair Practice** Work with a partner. Use the dialogue model in Activity 3 and the messages from Activity 4 to practice giving and taking messages.

because / so

Use *because* to tell the **reason** for something:
  I can't come to work **because I have the flu**.
Use *so* to tell the **result** of something:
  I have the flu **so I can't come to work**.

6 Write Complete the sentences with a reason and a result.

1. She wants to make a lot of money because _____ .

   She wants to make a lot of money so _____ .

2. They love their dog because _____ .

   They love their dog so _____ .

3. He bought a car because _____ .

   He bought a car so _____ .

4. He's going to Las Vegas because _____ .

   He's going to Las Vegas so _____ .

5. Lupe works as a cashier because _____ .

   Lupe works as a cashier so _____ .

7 Say It Practice the conversation with a partner.

turn off all the computers

A: Can you do me a big favor?

B: Sure. What is it?

A: Would you please <u>turn off all the computers</u> before you go home today?

B: No problem. I'll <u>turn them off</u> before I leave.

A: Great. Thank you.

Practice the conversation again. Use the photographs below.

1. hand out the paychecks

2. pick up the mail

3. wake up the security guard

Phrasal verbs

Phrasal verbs are verbs that have **two parts**: a **verb** and a **preposition**:
The meaning is usually different from the verb by itself.

Turn means "twist" or "go around." (Please **turn** the wheel.)

But **turn on / turn off** means "to switch on or off, operate" (**Turn off** the lights when you leave the room.)

Check Point:

✓ Most phrasal verbs are **separable**—you can use object pronouns between the two parts of the phrasal verb.

Would you pick up my son from school?

I'd be happy to **pick him up**. (correct)

I'd be happy to *pick up him*. (*not* correct)

8 Write Complete the sentences with phrasal verbs and object pronouns.

1. Would you please turn on the air conditioner?

   I'd be happy to _____ _____ _____ .

2. Don't forget to hand in your homework.

   I'll _____ _____ _____ at the end of class.

3. Could you drop Maria off at school tomorrow?

   No problem. I'll _____ _____ _____ at 8:00.

4. Please take off your hat when you come into the office.

   Sorry. I'll _____ _____ _____ right now.

5. Please wake up your little sister. It's almost 9:00.

   OK. I'll _____ _____ _____ right now.

9 Match Match the phrasal verbs with their meanings.

1. ___ put on   **a.** use a book or dictionary to find information

2. ___ drop off   **b.** wear clothes or jewelry

3. ___ bring back   **c.** stop sleeping

4. ___ wake up   **d.** deliver something or someone in a different

5. ___ look up   place

6. ___ run into   **e.** return

                       f. meet by accident

⑩ Problem Solving Look at Lupe's and Betsy's pay stubs. Answer the questions below.

```
┌──────────────────────────────────────────┐   ┌──────────────────────────────────────────┐
│         P A Y M E N T   R E C E I P T      │   │         P A Y M E N T   R E C E I P T      │
├──────────────────────────────────────────┤   ├──────────────────────────────────────────┤
│ Lupe Haro        │ GROSS PAY:.....$345.00 │   │ Betsy Diaz       │ GROSS PAY:.....$340.00 │
│ FOR THE WEEK OF: │ FEDERAL TAX:.....$32.00 │   │ FOR THE WEEK OF: │ FEDERAL TAX:.....$50.00 │
│ APRIL 17-23      │ STATE TAX:......$12.25  │   │ APRIL 17-23      │ STATE TAX:......$15.00  │
│ PAY RATE: $11.50 │ LOCAL TAX:..........$0  │   │ PAY RATE: $8.50  │ LOCAL TAX:..........$0  │
│        per hour  │ SSI:............$17.25   │   │        per hour  │ SSI:............$17.00   │
│                  │ NET PAY:  $283.50       │   │                  │ NET PAY:  $258.00       │
│ TOTAL: 30 HOURS  │ Medical: Employer paid. │   │ TOTAL: 40 HOURS  │ Medical: none.          │
│                  │ Exemptions: 4           │   │                  │ Exemptions: 1           │
└──────────────────────────────────────────┘   └──────────────────────────────────────────┘
```

1. How many hours did Lupe work? _____ .

2. How much was Lupe's take-home pay? _____ .

3. How much was Lupe's gross pay? _____ .

4. How much was withheld (= taken out, removed) for Lupe's social security (= SSI)? _____ .

5. How much is Betsy's hourly pay? _____ .

6. Who makes more per hour? _____ .

7. Who worked more hours this week? _____ .

8. Who made more money? _____ .

9. How much tax did Betsy pay? _____ .

10. Who paid more federal tax? Why? _____ .

⑪ Teamwork Task Work in teams of three or four. Look at the phrasal verbs in Activity 9. Work together to write questions and answers using the six phrasal verbs. Use object pronouns in your answers. Ask your questions to students from other teams.

Homework
Paycheck Stubs
Borrow a paycheck stub from someone you know or use one of your own. Bring it into class and tell the class all the information you can find on the stub except the person's name. Don't tell the class whose paycheck it is.

1 **Read and Listen** Read the story. Then listen to the story.

"Can We Talk?"

After her first month at her new job, Jessica received her first employee evaluation. Her supervisor, Ms. Clark, came to Jessica's desk. "I have your one-month employee evaluation," she said. "Can we talk after lunch?"

"Yes, of course," Jessica said.

Jessica worried for the next two hours. She didn't eat lunch. When she went to Ms. Clark's office at 1:00, her hands were shaking. She sat down on the other side of her supervisor's desk. Ms. Clark picked up an evaluation form. Jessica's face felt hot. "Is that one mine?" she asked.

Ms. Clark smiled. "Yes, it's yours. But don't worry. You're doing great."

"I am?"

Ms. Clark looked at the form. "Well, your attendance is perfect. You get along great with everyone. And you're a hard worker."

Jessica's hands stopped shaking. "Thank you," she said.

"There is one small problem," Ms. Clark said. "You came in late twice this month."

"I'm sorry about that," Jessica said. "The traffic was really bad a couple of mornings. I'll try to leave earlier."

"OK," Ms. Clark said. "Here's your evaluation. Keep up the good work."

"Thank you," Jessica said. "I will."

---

2 **Write** Read the sentences. Circle True or False.

1. After one month at her job Jessica received
   a performance review.   True   False

2. Ms. Clark was upset with Jessica's work.   True   False

3. Jessica's evaluation was perfect.   True   False

4. Jessica was nervous about her evaluation.   True   False

5. Jessica apologized for coming in late.   True   False

CRITICAL THINKING:

6. Do you think Ms. Clark is really happy with Jessica's work? Why or why not?

_____

③ Best Answer Bubble the correct answer.

1. She wears shorts to work. She has a problem with her _____.

   a) punctuality   **b)** attendance   **c)** appearance   ○   ○   ○

2. They are my friends. Please don't complain about _____.

   a) him   **b)** them   **c)** their   ○   ○   ○

3. He was alone in the room so he was talking to _____.

   a) him   **b)** himself   **c)** hisself   ○   ○   ○

4. Give that key to Bob and Cindy. It's _____.

   a) theirs   **b)** their   **c)** our   ○   ○   ○

5. She got a good job _____ she bought a new car.

   a) because   **b)** so   **c)** finally   ○   ○   ○

④ Write Read the problems. Write an offer to help for each problem.

1. Ralph needs help to move some large boxes.

   _____.

2. Lupe needs to get a price check for a can of soup.

   _____.

3. John and Laura need someone to help them paint their house next week.

   _____.

4. Manuel wants someone to pick up his paycheck from the office.

   _____.

5. Oscar doesn't know how to operate the copy machine.

   _____.

6. José needs to wake up really early on Saturday.

   _____.

⑤ Write Complete the conversation.

A: Can I talk to you in my office for a minute?

B: _____.

A: Please, sit down.

B: _____.

A: I see we have a couple of problems on your employee evaluation. First, you came in very late last Monday.

B: Yes, _____ ,

_____ . I was late

_____ .

A: That's a good reason. But there also is a problem with your appearance. The evaluation says that sometimes you don't dress very well.

B: _____ .

A: OK. Please try. It's important.

6 Pair Practice Practice the conversation in Activity 5 with a partner.

7 Teamwork Task Work in teams of three. Student 1 is an employee. Student 2 is an office assistant. Student 3 is their supervisor.

1. Employee: Call the office assistant. Tell him or her that you are going to be late for work today. Apologize. Give the reason why you'll be late. Tell him or her what time you expect to arrive.

2. Office Assistant: Write down the message. Call the supervisor and give him or her the message.

3. Supervisor: Read the message. Call the employee into your office. Tell him or her it's the fourth time he or she has been late this month.

4. Employee: Go to the supervisor's office. Tell the boss the reason(s) for your lateness. Apologize for this problem. Tell him or her you will try to do better.

Practice the role play with your team. Then perform it for the class.

Pronunciation Reductions: *him* and *her* become *'im* and *'er*
Many native speakers drop beginning sounds when they use the object pronouns *him* and *her*. For example, *Pick him up* becomes *Pick 'im up.*

A. Listen and repeat the following sentences:
Please drop him off at work.
Wake her up at 8:00.
Bring her back after class.
Pick him up at school.

B. Work with a partner. Take turns reading the sentences to each other. Say *'im* and *'er* instead of *him* and *her*.

Be positive! Be punctual!

Do you want to learn a few tips—suggestions—to improve your job performance? Do a search for job performance tips. Which tip or tips do you think are the most important? Which ones do you need to work on? Which ones do you do well? Share your ideas with a partner or a small group.

I can . . .			
• ask for and offer help.	1	2	3
• accept and decline help.	1	2	3
• describe steps in a process.	1	2	3
• request a schedule change.	1	2	3
• use object, reflexive, and possessive pronouns.	1	2	3
• use phrasal verbs.	1	2	3
• use because and so.	1	2	3
• use someone, anyone, everyone, and no one.	1	2	3
• read an employee evaluation form.	1	2	3
• give and respond to criticism.	1	2	3
• give and take telephone messages.	1	2	3
• make and respond to requests.	1	2	3
• read a paycheck stub.	1	2	3

1 = not well   2 = OK   3 = very well

8 Write Write the missing words in the cartoon story. Use these words: *First, Then, anybody, I'll, everyone, himself, raise, Evaluation, attendance, him, punctuality, show.*

Alberto: Does (1)_____ need any help? How about Manuel?
Boss: No, he'd rather do it by (2)_____.

Boss: Why don't you help José. He doesn't know how to look up that information very well.
Alberto: No problem. I'll (3)_____ (4)_____ how.

Alberto: OK. (5)_____, you have to click on the icon. (6)_____ you have to type your password.

LATER THAT SAME DAY...

Alberto: Mr. Carter, if I want to get married, I'm going to need more money. So, I have to ask you for a (7)_____.

Boss: Well, Alberto, I have your Employee (8)_____. It says that you get along well with (9)_____, and that you are a hard worker. But you have a problem with (10)_____. And your (11)_____ isn't so good either.

Alberto: Does that mean ... no raise?
Boss: I'm afraid so. Not this year. I'm sorry.
Alberto: Me, too. But (12)_____ try to improve. Thank you.

9 Pair Practice Practice the cartoon story with a partner.

A Better Job

GOALS

- ✓ Talk about past jobs
- ✓ Describe skills and abilities
- ✓ Read "Help Wanted" ads
- ✓ Fill out a job application
- ✓ Review verb tenses
- ✓ Use *(be) able to*
- ✓ Use the simple past and past continuous
- ✓ Use personality adjectives
- ✓ Understand nonverbal behavior
- ✓ Discuss salary, benefits, and working conditions
- ✓ Ask and answer job interview questions

What position are you interested in? ⑤

④ CURRICULUM VITAE

ANN PAGE
PERSONNEL DIRE...

⑩ **I'm outgoing and very dependable.**

⑨ **I'm a hard worker and I'm very good at supervising people.**

① **Read and Listen** *Read the story. Look at the pictures. Listen to the story. Then match the words with the numbers in the pictures.*

The Job Interview

Alex is applying for a job as a warehouse manager for a big electronics company. He filled out an application and brought his résumé to the interview. He gave the interviewer a firm handshake when she introduced herself to him. Then, as she interviewed him, he kept eye contact with her.

The interviewer asked him about his experience and his skills. After he talked about his skills, she said, "Tell me about your personal interests. How would you describe yourself?" He told her some things about himself. Then she asked why she should hire him. He gave her some good reasons. At the end of the interview, he said, "I'd like to be your next warehouse manager." He hoped he sounded like a supervisor!

_____ résumé
_____ interviewer
_____ firm handshake
_____ job applicant
_____ eye contact
_____ your experience
_____ your strengths and abilities
_____ the job you want
_____ your skills
_____ your personality

curriculum vitae = résumé

183

Skills and Abilities

1 **Say It** Practice the conversation with a partner.

***Daily Fashion Magazine* / 2 ½ years**

A: What kind of job are you looking for?

B: I want to be a <u>receptionist</u>.

A: Do you have any experience?

B: Yes, I do. I worked as a <u>receptionist</u> for *Daily Fashion Magazine* for <u>two and a half years</u>.

A: Great. Do you want to fill out an application?

B: Yes, please. Thank you.

Practice the conversation again. Use the pictures below.

1. **Downtown Department Store / 3 years**

2. **The Big Tire Company / 6 years**

3. **The Spaghetti Company / 18 months**

2 **Write** Write short answers to the following questions.

1. Do you have a car?   No, _____.

2. Can you drive a truck?   Yes, _____.

3. Can you start next week?   No, _____.

4. Would you like to come in for an interview?   Yes, _____.

5. Did you have a job in your country?   No, _____.

6. Are you willing to work on weekends?   Yes, _____.

7. Were you living in the same place last year?   Yes, _____.

8. Can we contact your previous employer?   Yes, _____.

> would you like to = can you
> are you willing to = can you / do you mind
> contact = call

3 **Say It** Practice the conversation with a partner.

answer phones and take messages / file

A: What skills do you have for the job?

B: You mean what can I do?

A: Yes, exactly.

B: Well, I can <u>answer phones and take messages</u>. And I am able to <u>file</u>, too.

A: Is that what you did on your last job?

B: I <u>answered phones</u> and <u>took messages</u>, but I <u>didn't file</u>. That wasn't part of my last job.

Practice the conversation again. Use the pictures below.

1. **do tune-ups and repair brakes / fix flat tires**

2. **plan menus and make Italian food / bake desserts**

3. **write contracts and do taxes / go to court**

GRAMMAR CHECK

(be) able to

Use *be* + *able to* for ability in the present, past, or future:

Present   I **am able to** speak three languages. =
           I **can** speak three languages.

Past   I **was able to** run fast when I was a teenager. =
           I **could** run fast when I was a teenager.

Future   I **will be able to** speak fluent English next year.

Check Points:
   ✓ You can use *be* + *able to* in place of *can* in the present.
   ✓ You can use *was / were able to* in place of *could* in the past.

4 **Write** Rewrite the sentences below. Change *can* or *could* to *be* + *able to*.

1. Helen can type fifty words per minute. _____ .

2. Monica could play the piano when she was three years old. _____ .

3. Can you ride a motorcycle? _____ .

4. Jack and Jill can sing very well. _____ .

5. Could you speak English two years ago? _____ .

5 **Pair Practice** Work with a partner. Ask and answer the questions about skills or abilities.

1. Were you able to speak English five years ago?

2. Are you able to drive a car?

3. At what age were you able to ride a bicycle?

4. Are you able to cook Chinese food?

5. Is your teacher able to speak Spanish?

6. Are you able to play a musical instrument?

7. Are your parents able to speak two languages?

8. Will you be able to pass your final exam?

9. What were you able to do in the past that you can't do now?

10. What will you be able to do in the future that you can't do now?

> Note: Skills or abilities refer to things that only some people are able to do. Usually they require training or practice.
> **Example:** Playing the guitar is a skill. Listening to music is not a skill. Anyone can do it.
> Skills or abilities you can use on your job are *job skills*.

6 **Write** Complete the chart. Decide if each activity is a job skill or not a job skill.

	A JOB SKILL	NOT A JOB SKILL
1. Repair appliances?		
2. Drive a truck?		
3. Watch TV?		
4. Eat Chinese food?		
5. Sew?		
6. Speak fluent English?		

Word Help: Reading classified ads
Required means that a skill or amount of experience is *necessary* to apply for the job. Here are other words used in classified ads that mean *required (req.)*:

must / a must	**need / needed**
minimum	**necessary**

Here are words used when a skill is important for the job, but not necessary to apply:

preferred (pref.)	**a plus**
desired	**helpful**

job = position = opening

7 **Listen** Listen for skills or abilities that are required for the jobs below. Then complete the "Help Wanted" ads.

WANTED: Full-Time Salesperson
_____ experience, pref. _____, energetic person, good _____ skills required, must be able to _____ _____. Start immediately. M–F 2:00 PM–10:00 PM (818) 555-6534

WANTED: Teacher's Aide
Must be able to _____ _____, good _____ necessary, pref. patient, friendly person, _____ literacy req. Part-time M–F, 8 AM–12 PM. Apply in person: The West Valley School.

8 **Write** Answer the questions about the classified ads in Activity 7.

1. Which job requires experience? How much experience? _____

2. What skills are required for the salesperson job? _____

3. What must you be able to do for this job? _____

4. What kind of person are they looking for? _____

5. What is the work schedule? _____

6. What skills are necessary for the teacher's aide position? _____

7. What must you be able to do? _____

8. What else is required? _____

9. How can you apply for the teacher's aide position? _____

10. How can you apply for the salesperson job? _____

9 **Pair Practice** Work with a partner. Write a classified ad for a job you want. Then write an ad for a job your partner wants. Include the job title and work schedule. Include what experience and skills are necessary. Include how to apply for the job.

10 **Teamwork Task** Work in teams of three or four. Make a list of skills that the members of your team has. Then circle the skills they can use on a job.

STUDENT 1	STUDENT 2	STUDENT 3	STUDENT 4
_____	_____	_____	_____
_____	_____	_____	_____
_____	_____	_____	_____
_____	_____	_____	_____

Homework

Read the classified ads section of a local newspaper. Find three jobs that require skills, abilities, or experience. Write the job title and the requirements for each job.

Job Applications

 Say It Practice the conversation with a partner.

```
JOB APPLICATION
     Work History
POSITION #1  TRUCK DRIVER
DUTIES  DRIVE A TRUCK / DELIVER GROCERIES
DATES WORKED  5/02 – 6/05
POSITION #2  TAXI DRIVER
DUTIES  DRIVE A TAXI / PICK UP PASSENGERS
DATES WORKED  5/00 – 4/02
```

A: What was your last job?

B: I was a <u>truck driver</u>.

A: What did you do on that job?

B: I <u>drove a truck</u>, and I <u>delivered groceries</u>.

A: What were you doing before that?

B: From <u>May, 2000 to April, 2002</u> I worked as a <u>taxi driver</u>.

A: What did you do on that job?

B: I <u>drove a taxi</u> and <u>picked up passengers</u>.

Practice the conversation again. Use the information below.

1.
```
JOB APPLICATION
     Work History
POSITION #1  Sales Clerk  DATES WORKED 02/02–03/05
DUTIES  sell men's clothes and
men's and women's shoes
POSITION #2  Sales Assistant  DATES WORKED 05/01–01/02
DUTIES  hang up clothes, take
inventory, help sales clerks
```

2.
```
JOB APPLICATION
     Work History
POSITION #1  Parking Attendant  DATES WORKED 04/03–09/05
DUTIES  Park cars and collect parking fees
POSITION #2  Security Guard  DATES WORKED 10/02–04/03
DUTIES  ride in delivery trucks and guard
the driver
```

GRAMMAR CHECK

Review of past continuous vs. simple past

In sentences that contain both the simple past and the past continuous, the past continuous action started first and was interrupted by the simple past action:

$\xrightarrow{\hspace{4cm} \text{X} \hspace{4cm}}$

I was cooking dinner   when she **called.**

↑   ↑

one action was going on—   then was interrupted by the other—
use past continuous   use simple past.

2 Write Complete the sentences with past continuous or simple past verbs.

1. (walk) She met her teacher while she _____ in the park.
2. (see) He was jogging when he _____ her.
3. (hear) Jim was watching TV when he _____ about the fire.
4. (travel) They got married while they _____ in Europe.
5. (call) They were eating dinner when her brother _____ from New York.
6. (find/clean) He _____ the money while he _____ the house.
7. (drive/have) While I _____ to work I _____ a small accident.

3 Write Answer the questions about the job application.

```
┌─────────────────────────────────────────────────────────────────────────┐
│                        APPLICATION FOR EMPLOYMENT                          │
│  Personal      NAME: Last  Martinez      First  Christina   Middle Initial I│
│  Information   STREET ADDRESS: 225 Lake St.   CITY: Chicago    STATE: IL    │
│   ZIP: 60606   HOW LONG HAVE YOU                                            │
│                LIVED AT THIS ADDRESS? 2 years   TEL. NO. (312) 555-3789     │
│  Education     LAST SCHOOL                                                   │
│                ATTENDED: Kennedy High School   LOCATION: Chicago, IL        │
│                DATES: 9/98 to 6/02   LAST GRADE COMPLETED: 12  GRADUATED: Yes│
│  Work          EMPLOYER: The Big Market  LOCATION: Chicago, IL  TEL. NO.: (312)555-8586│
│  History       SUPERVISOR: Tomas Lopez  DATES WORKED: 9/04-Present  JOB TITLE: Deli Clerk│
│  DUTIES: make sandwiches, serve hot food                                    │
│  Work          EMPLOYER: The Little Market  LOCATION: Chicago, IL  TEL. NO.: (312)555-3485│
│  History       SUPERVISOR: Ms Lucy Jones  DATES WORKED: 2/02-8/03  JOB TITLE: Counter Person│
│  DUTIES: sell bakery goods, make and sell coffee drinks                     │
│  Availability  FULL-TIME: YES  PART-TIME: NO  WEEKENDS: YES  EVENINGS: YES  │
└─────────────────────────────────────────────────────────────────────────┘
```

1. Whose application is it? _____.
2. Where does she live? _____.
3. When did she move there? _____.
4. What is her job now? _____.
5. What did she do on her last job? _____.
6. What was she doing in 2001? _____.
7. How long did she work at The Little Market? _____.
8. What does she do on her present job? _____.
9. What was she doing in January of 2003? _____.
10. When can she work? _____.

Listen Listen and fill in the missing information on Lin's application form.

APPLICATION FOR EMPLOYMENT

Personal Information

NAME: Last **Tran** First **Lin** Middle Initial **T**

STREET ADDRESS: **Park Ave.** CITY: **Los Angeles** STATE: **CA**

ZIP: _____ HOW LONG HAVE YOU LIVED AT THIS ADDRESS? _____ TEL. NO.: ( )**555-3789**

Education

LAST SCHOOL ATTENDED: **West Valley Adult School** LOCATION: **Los Angeles, CA**

DATES: _____ DEGREE: **None**

Work History

EMPLOYER: **Nation's Bank** LOCATION: **Van Nuys, CA** TEL. NO.: **(818) 555-8586**

SUPERVISOR: **Brenda Smith** DATES WORKED: _____ JOB TITLE: _____

DUTIES: **cash checks, make change, help customers at the teller window**

Work History

EMPLOYER: **The Auto Import Co.** LOCATION: **Hue, Vietnam** TEL. NO.: _____

SUPERVISOR: **Thuy Nguyen** DATES WORKED: _____ JOB TITLE: **Accountant**

DUTIES: **wrote payroll checks for** _____ **and** _____ **company bills**

Availability

FULL-TIME: _____ PART-TIME: **No** WEEKENDS: _____ EVENINGS: **No**

---

5 **Write** Write ten questions about Lin's job application form. Use these question words: *Whose, When, Where, What, How many, How long, Can, Who, Does,* and *Was.*

Example: Whose application is it?

1. _____ ?
2. _____ ?
3. _____ ?
4. _____ ?
5. _____ ?
6. _____ ?
7. _____ ?
8. _____ ?
9. _____ ?
10. _____ ?

6 **Pair Practice** Work with a partner. Ask your partner the questions you wrote about Lin Tran for Activity 5.

7 **Teamwork Task** Work in teams of four. Student 1 is a job applicant. The other three students help Student 1 fill out his or her job application. Student 2: Complete the Personal Information section of the application for Student 1. (Ask him or her questions and write what he or she tells you.) Student 3: Complete the Education and Availability sections for Student 1. Student 4: Complete the Work History section for Student 1. (If Student 1 never had a job, talk about a pretend job or pretend that English class is your job.)

APPLICATION FOR EMPLOYMENT

Personal Information

NAME: _____ Last _____ First _____ Middle Initial

STREET ADDRESS: _____ CITY: _____ STATE: ___

ZIP: _____ HOW LONG HAVE YOU LIVED AT THIS ADDRESS? _____ TEL. NO.: ( ) _____

Education

LAST SCHOOL ATTENDED: _____ LOCATION: _____

DATES: _____ DEGREE: _____

Work History

EMPLOYER: _____ LOCATION: _____ TEL. NO.: _____

SUPERVISOR: _____ DATES WORKED: _____ JOB TITLE: _____

DUTIES: _____

Work History

EMPLOYER: _____ LOCATION: _____ TEL. NO.: _____

SUPERVISOR: _____ DATES WORKED: _____ JOB TITLE: _____

DUTIES: _____

Availability FULL-TIME: _____ PART-TIME: _____ WEEKENDS: _____ EVENINGS: _____

The Interview

1 **Read** Read the e-mail from Jessica's friend Luis. Circle any words you don't understand.

Hi Jessica,

It was nice to hear from you. I have good news, too. Last week they made me the manager here. I am in charge of the whole store! I'll make more money, and I'll have better benefits and more responsibility. Now I have to hire someone for my old job. I interviewed four people today.

First, I interviewed a woman named Alicia. She seemed bright and friendly. But I think she might not be very honest. Some of her answers in the interview didn't match her résumé and her job application. For this job she will be working with cash registers and money, so honesty is important.

The second person, David, was polite and seemed like a fast learner, but he wasn't punctual. He arrived 10 minutes late for the interview!

The third one, Rosanna, was punctual and outgoing. She seemed very creative. She had a lot of interesting, new ideas. And she gave examples of how she is organized and dependable, too. These are important skills for the job.

Finally, I interviewed Robert. He was organized and on time. But he was very quiet. He didn't smile or make eye contact with me, so I think he might be too shy for this job.

I think Rosanna is the best person for the job. What do you think?

Your friend,

Luis

2 **Write** Write *same* next to each pair of words that have the same, or almost the same meanings. Write *different* next to each pair that have opposite, or very different meanings. Use your dictionary if necessary.

1. friendly—outgoing _____
2. punctual—late _____
3. bright—fast learner _____
4. outgoing—shy _____
5. dependable—reliable _____
6. polite—nice _____
7. organized—creative _____
8. dishonest—honest _____
9. in charge of—not responsible for _____

3 **Write** Complete the sentences with reasons. Reread Luis's e-mail if necessary.

1. Alicia isn't honest because _____

   _____.

2. David isn't punctual because _____

   _____.

3. Rosanna is creative because _____

   _____.

4. Robert is shy because _____

   _____.

5. Luis has to be responsible because _____

   _____.

CRITICAL THINKING:

Find two or three adjectives in the e-mail in Activity 1 that describe you. Give a reason why.

I think I am _____ because _____

_____.

I think I am _____ because _____

_____.

4 **Say It** Practice the conversation with a partner.

keep things neat and always know where everything is

A: Tell me a little about yourself.

B: You mean about my skills and experience?

A: No. I can see that on your application form. Tell me about your personality. What are your personal strengths?

B: Well, I think I'm <u>organized</u> because I <u>keep things neat and I always know where everything is</u>.

A: That's a good quality. I'm happy to hear that.

Practice the conversation again. Use the pictures below.

1. **like to meet and talk to new people**

2. **do what I say I'm going to do**

3. **understand new things quickly**

⑤ Group Practice *Find someone who . . .* Work in a large group or with the whole class. Try to find students who say *yes* to the questions below. If a student says *yes*, write the student's name on the line and write a reason why he or she said *yes*. Then ask the next question to a different student.

	NAME	REASON
1. Are you punctual?	_____	_____
2. Are you outgoing?	_____	_____
3. Are you a fast learner?	_____	_____
4. Are you creative?	_____	_____
5. Are you organized?	_____	_____

Word Help: Nonverbal Communication

Nonverbal communication = what you "say" about yourself without speaking through body language and behavior

Body language includes:
- **posture**: how you hold your body when you stand or sit
- **grooming**: how you cut your hair, fix your nails, trim your beard or mustache, etc.
- **dress**: what kind of clothes, makeup, jewelry you wear, and other things you wear or show, like tattoos

Behavior includes:
- **Eye contact**: how you meet or don't meet the other person's eyes
- **Handshake**: how you shake or don't shake the other person's hand
- **Smile**: when or how often you smile

Remember these tips:
- Don't smoke.
- Don't chew gum.
- Pay attention when the interviewer is speaking.
- Smile, shake hands, and look the interviewer in the eyes when you greet him or her.

Culture Tip

Nonverbal Communication

Nonverbal communication is important in interviews. Between 80% and 90% of the communication at a job interview is nonverbal. So sit up straight and smile! ☺

6 **Write** What's wrong with this picture? Look at the picture of the job interview. Make a list of problems you see. Write as many things as you can. Correct what he is doing wrong: *He should not be . . .*

_____

_____

_____

_____

_____

Word Help Salary, Benefits, and Working Conditions
In addition to the job title and job duties, there are other things that make a job a "good job." Salary, benefits, and working conditions are also important.
salary: any pay you receive from a job
benefits: anything you get that isn't money
working conditions: all the good or bad things about your workplace

7 **Group Practice** Work in a group of three or four. Put the following list in the correct categories:

health insurance	hourly pay	paid holidays
friendly coworkers	a 9-to-5 schedule	a nice boss
a clean safe workplace	overtime hours	opportunity to advance
a holiday bonus	paid vacation	tips
a retirement plan		

SALARY	**BENEFITS**	**WORKING CONDITIONS**
_____	_____	_____
_____	_____	_____
_____	_____	_____
_____	_____	_____
_____	_____	_____

8 **Teamwork Task** Work in teams of three or four. Discuss the list of salary, benefits, and working conditions above. Decide which are the most important for your team. Rank them from the most important (1) to the least important (13). Then tell the class which three or four you think are the most important.

1. _____
2. _____
3. _____
4. _____
5. _____

6. _____
7. _____
8. _____
9. _____
10. _____

11. _____
12. _____
13. _____

Game Time

Find Your Match

Your teacher will give you a piece of paper with a job title or a job skill. If you have a job title (auto mechanic), you must find the other student who has the matching job skill (I can fix cars). Ask "What can you do?" to find a skill. Ask "What do you do?" to find a job title. Stand up, walk around the room, ask the right question, and find your match!

 Read and Listen Read the story. Then listen to the story.

Thinking Ahead

Jessica likes her job, but she knows that people change jobs a lot in the United States. Sometimes it is necessary to change jobs to get a higher salary or an opportunity to advance. Right now Jessica is happy with her salary. She gets along well with her coworkers, and she likes her boss. Her job is in a very nice location. But her job doesn't have very good benefits. They don't provide health insurance or paid vacation. And there isn't much opportunity for advancement, so in the future she might look and apply for another job.

When she goes on another job interview, she will talk about her computer animation skills and her artistic ability. She can also say that she is a good team player, and that she is very organized and dependable. Sometimes she isn't very punctual, but she won't tell them that!

✏ Write

1. Why do people sometimes change jobs? _____
2. Is Jessica happy with her pay? _____
3. What job skills does Jessica have? _____
4. What other personal strengths does Jessica have? _____
5. What is one of Jessica's weaknesses? _____
6. Does Jessica's job have good working conditions? Why or why not? ____

_____

CRITICAL THINKING:

7. Do you think Jessica has a good job? Why or why not? _____

_____

✏ Write
Write an e-mail to Jessica. Tell her that you are looking for a job. Tell her about your current job or activities. Tell her about your skills, experience, and personal strengths. Also, tell her about any weaknesses you have. Ask her for advice.

4 **Best Answer** Bubble the correct answer.   a   b   c

1. Were you living at this address last year? Yes, I _____.

   a) did   **b)** was   **c)** am   ○   ○   ○

2. What skills do you have for this job? I am _____
   repair plumbing problems.

   a) can   **b)** know how   **c)** able to   ○   ○   ○

3. _____ did you leave that job? Last October.

   a) When   **b)** Where   **c)** Why   ○   ○   ○

4. She always does what she says. She's really _____.

   a) organized   **b)** polite   **c)** dependable   ○   ○   ○

5. I think I am _____ because I enjoy meeting and
   talking to people.

   a) shy   **b)** outgoing   **c)** reliable   ○   ○   ○

5 **Write** Complete the conversation with your information.

A: Do you have any experience?

B: _____

A: What job skills do you have?

B: _____

A: Tell me about your personality. What are your personal strengths?

B: _____

A: What job benefits and working conditions are important to you?

B: _____

A: Do you have any questions for me?

B: Yes. _____

6 **Pair Practice** Work with a partner. Ask and answer the questions in
Activity 5.

7 Write What is it? Write a description under each picture.

1. _____

2. _____

3. _____

8 Listen Listen to the conversations and fill in the missing information on the "Help Wanted" ads.

Office Assistant

Temp. Job, Medical Office. _____

_____ type 25 wpm.

1+ year _____ .

Good _____ .

Must be a _____ .

✸ Receptionist ✸

Import/Export. Must be

_____ and _____ .

_____ include greeting customers, filing, answering phones. Prefer a

_____ with

good _____ .

9 Teamwork Task Work in teams of five or six. Ask your teammates about their personal strengths. For example, "Are you punctual?" If your teammates say, "Yes", ask why they think they are punctual. On a scale of 1–5, ask them to rate themselves (1 is the low end—not very punctual, and 5 is on the high end—always punctual). Decide together who is the most punctual member of your team. Then ask about the other qualities.

NAME OF TEAM MEMBER	PUNCTUAL	OUTGOING	ORGANIZED	DEPENDABLE	NON-VERBAL SKILLS (POSTURE, GROOMING, DRESS)

The most punctual member of our team is _____ .

The most outgoing member of our team is _____ .

The most organized member of our team is _____ .

The most dependable member of our team is _____ .

The best-groomed member of our team is _____ .

Pronunciation Stressing content words

In English, the most important words in a sentence get more stress than the other words. We call these important words *content words*. They are said louder and often at a higher pitch than the other words.

A. Listen and repeat the following sentences:
Do you want an application?
Eye contact is important.
I drove a truck.
I want to be a receptionist.
Can you work on weekends?

B. Listen again. This time <u>underline</u> the content words in these sentences.

C. Now work with a partner. Practice one of the conversations in this chapter. As you speak, be sure to stress the content words.

INTERNET IDEA
Looking for jobs
Search the Internet for information on jobs available in your community. Start with the classified ads in your local paper. Tell your class about the kinds of jobs you found, and which one(s) you liked, didn't like, have enough experience to do, etc.

I can . . .			
• talk about past jobs.	1	2	3
• describe skills and abilities.	1	2	3
• read "Help Wanted" ads.	1	2	3
• fill out a job application.	1	2	3
• review verb tenses.	1	2	3
• use (be) able to.	1	2	3
• use the simple past and past continuous.	1	2	3
• use personality adjectives.	1	2	3
• understand nonverbal behavior.	1	2	3
• discuss salary, benefits, and working conditions.	1	2	3
• ask and answer job interview questions.	1	2	3

1 = not well   2 = OK   3 = very well

DOWNTOWN

⑩ **Write** Write the missing words in the cartoon story. Use these words: *benefits, full-time, dependable, salary, working conditions, skills, hard worker, fill out, going to, spoke, how.*

Alberto: I'm afraid I'm not
(1)_____ get that raise,
Cindy. I (2)_____ to the boss
this morning.

Alberto: He said I might be able to get
a raise next year.
Cindy: Well, maybe you can
(3)_____ some applications and
find a higher paying job.

Cindy: You are a (4)_____ and you're
very (5)_____ . You have a lot of good
(6)_____ . I'm sure a lot of companies
would be happy to have you.
Alberto: That's true. But I don't really want a
new job.

Cindy: Then you don't need a new job.
Your job has good (7)_____ and
you like the (8)_____ .
Alberto: That's true, too.

Alberto: But here's the problem. If I don't get
a raise, (9)_____ can we afford a nice
wedding and a beautiful honeymoon?
Cindy: Well, I can look for a (10)_____
job with a higher (11)_____ . And as for
the honeymoon . . .

Cindy: I would be happy to spend our
honeymoon here in L.A. The important
thing is to be together.
Alberto: Thank you for understanding!

⑪ **Pair Practice** Practice the story with a partner.

Chapter 1:
Personal Information

Page 3 (Chapter Opening)

Listen *Listen and repeat each word. Then point to each item in the picture.*

a chalkboard
a country
a nationality
an eraser
a piece of chalk
a pencil sharpener
classmates
a handshake
uncle
aunt
bald
cousins
short gray hair
blond hair
dark curly hair
hobby
a work schedule
a supervisor
tall and thin
short and heavy
coworkers

Page 5 (Lesson 1, Activity 5)

Listen *Listen to the conversation between Hong Yu and the school counselor. Write the missing information in Hong Yu's student registration form.*

Man: What's your name?
Woman: My name is Wang Hong Yu.
Man: Which one is your last name?
Woman: My last name is Wang. W-a-n-g.
Man: And your address?
Woman: I live at 315 Spring Street.
Man: Is that in Pasadena?
Woman: Yes. Pasadena, California. My zip code is 91305.
Man: And your telephone number?
Woman: My area code is 626. And the number is…555-2987.
Man: What is your date of birth?
Woman: My birthday is May 15th.
Man: And the year?
Woman: 1982.
Man: And where were you born?
Woman: In Hong Kong, China.

Page 16 (Lesson 3, Activity 11)

Listen *Listen to the conversations. Write the correct words under each picture. Use these phrases: watch TV, read books, go to the movies, jog, play cards, and bake.*

Woman 1: What do you like to do in your free time, Matt?
Man 1: Me? Actually, I don't have any hobbies. Most of my free time I just watch TV. Oh, is that a hobby?
Woman 1: How about you Mara? What do you like to do on weekends?
Woman 2: My favorite thing? Well, I really like to read books.
Woman 1: How about you, Hong Yu?
Woman 3: I love movies. When I have extra time, I usually go to the movies.
Woman 1: How about you, Mr. Ryan?
Man 2: I jog. When I have free time, I like to jog a few miles.
Woman 1: Tania, what do you like to do?
Woman 4: I like to play cards. I get together with friends and we play cards.
Woman 1: What about Alexa? What does she like to do?
Woman 4: Believe it or not, she likes to bake.
Woman 1: Bake?
Woman 4: Bake! She bakes delicious cakes and pies. You have to try them!
Woman 1: I'd love to.

Page 17 (Chapter 1 Review, Activity 1)

Read and Listen *Read the story. Then listen to the story.*

NEW IN TOWN

Jessica is twenty-four years old and new in town. She was born in Colombia, South America, but she lives in the United States now. She lives in Los Angeles, California. In her new home, she lives with her uncle, her aunt, and her two cousins. She doesn't know them well, but she likes them very much.

In Colombia, Jessica was an artist, but the pay wasn't very good. Now she is a computer animator and the pay is *very* good. She misses her parents and her brother and sister, but she is excited about her new life in the U.S. She also has a new school where she is studying English. She has some very interesting classmates. One is Russian. She was a dancer in her country. Another is Italian. He was a soccer player in his country for ten years.

Jessica has a lot of hobbies. She likes to ski in the winter and she likes to hike in the summer. She also likes to ride her bicycle and dance. But she doesn't have much free time for hobbies right now. For now, her job is her hobby!

Page 20 (Chapter 1 Review)

Pronunciation *Wh- question intonation*

A. Your voice goes up at the end of *yes/no* questions.

Do you know him?   Is he thin?
At the end of a Wh- question, your voice goes up a little and then down.
What do you want?   Who are you looking for?

B. *Listen and draw the arrow. Listen again and repeat.*

What do you want?	When do you leave on vacation?
Who are you looking for?	Why do you want to know?
Where are we meeting?	How long were you a teacher?

Chapter 2:
Daily Activities

Page 23 (Chapter Opening)

Listen *Listen and repeat each word. Then point to each item in the picture.*

cooking
delivering mail
washing dishes
cutting hair
doing laundry
making a bed
paying bills
watering the garden
a café
a hair salon
a clothing store
a hairstylist
a salesperson
a customer
letters
a package
priority mail
making coffee

Page 25 (Lesson 1, Activity 5)

Listen *Listen to the conversation. Correct any mistakes in Activity 4.*

Man: Do you have a lot to do today?
Woman: Of course. I have a lot to do every Saturday.
Man: What do you do every Saturday?
Woman: Well, first, I make breakfast. Then I do the shopping. Then I start to do the housework. I make the beds and do the dishes, and at the same time I do the laundry, and sometimes make a phone call or two. In the afternoon I go to the gym for an hour to do some exercises, then I take a shower. Then I make a decision about what I'm going to make for dinner. Then I cook the food and feed the kids. Sometimes I make a cake for dessert. After dinner I try to help my children do their homework.
Man: You are busy! What about your husband? What does he do all day Saturday?
Woman: He goes to work and makes money!
Man: Oh, well that's important, too!

Listen *Listen to the conversations. Write the names of the places you hear on the map below.*

Woman: Where is the supermarket?

Man: It's on Hollywood Boulevard, next to the drugstore.

Man: Excuse me. Where is the bank?

Woman: It's on Hollywood Boulevard, across from the post office.

Man: Thank you.

Woman: Excuse me. I'm trying to find the health club.

Man: It's on Hollywood and New York, next to the post office.

Woman: Thanks.

Man: You're welcome.

Man: Pardon me, miss, do you know where the video store is?

Woman: Yes, it's on Hollywood Boulevard, between the school and the pizza shop.

Woman: Excuse me. I'm trying to find the hair salon. Do you know where it is?

Man: I certainly do. It's on the corner of Sunset and California, next to a wonderful Chinese restaurant.

Woman: Thank you very much.

Man: Wait! Um, would you like to have lunch at the Chinese restaurant?

Woman: No, thank you. I'm already late.

Man: Maybe some other time?

Woman (Annoyed): Good-bye, sir!

Read and listen *Read the story. Then listen to the story.*

Jessica's New Neighborhood

Jessica's home life in the United States is not very different from her life at home in Colombia. The housework is the same. She does most of the same household chores. The biggest difference is that in Colombia, Jessica's mother did the laundry and cooked for the whole family.

But Jessica's new neighborhood is very different. There are many stores, restaurants, and businesses she can walk to in her neighborhood. She could eat a different kind of food every day if she had the money. There is a Japanese restaurant across the street, a café right next door, a pizza shop, a Chinese restaurant, and a supermarket nearby. There is also a hotel with an American restaurant inside. Jessica sometimes thinks that Americans like to eat, but they don't often like to cook.

A lot of Jessica's friends and classmates work in her neighborhood. Her friend Vida cuts hair in the hair salon. Tania sells clothes in a small boutique. Cindy works in a coffee shop or café. And Rosa is a personal trainer in the health club.

Some of Jessica's neighbors go to the health club. They exercise there three or four times a week. Maybe they have to exercise a lot because there are so many restaurants nearby!

Pronunciation *Present tense s endings*
Present tense verbs that follow he, she, and it end in the letter s. However, this s ending has three different pronunciations. It can sound like s, z, or iz.

A. *Listen and repeat these sentences. Listen to the s ending.*

Sounds like s	She cooks dinner.
Sounds like z	She pays the bills.
Sounds like iz	She washes the dishes.

B. *You will hear nine verbs. Listen for the s endings. Write each verb in the correct column.*

1. makes, makes
2. pays, pays
3. washes, washes
4. drinks, drinks
5. feeds, feeds
6. gets, gets
7. cashes, cashes
8. buys, buys
9. exercises, exercises

Chapter 3: **Food**

Page 43 (Chapter Opening)

Listen *Listen and repeat each word. Then point to each item in the picture.*

napkins
cabinet
salad
kitchen table
refrigerator
counter
freezer
stuffing
silverware
apple pie
glasses
mashed potatoes
ice cream
cheese
coffee
tea
sweet potatoes
milk
corn
dishes
bread
soda
candles
turkey
cookies
plates
bowls
ice
butter

Page 48 (Lesson 2, Activity 3)

Listen *Listen to the conversations and check your answers to Activity 2.*

Man: What do we need from the market?
Woman: We need some bread.
Woman: Why is she going into that supermarket?
Man: She wants to buy an apple.
Man: What are you going to cook?
Woman: I'm going to cook some spaghetti
Man: Great.
Woman: What else do we need for the soup?
Man: We need to buy some mushrooms and an onion.
Man: What's he going to buy?
Woman: He's going to buy some oranges and some beans.
Man: Excellent.
Man: What are they going to cook?
Woman: They're going to cook an eggplant.

Page 49 (Lesson 2, Activity 4)

Listen *Listen and circle the beverages you hear. Then tell the class what Jessica's family likes to drink.*

Jessica: Everybody in my family likes to drink different things at different times of day. My uncle, for example, always drinks coffee in the morning. But the rest of the day he drinks cola or root beer. My aunt never drinks coffee or cola. She drinks juice. She usually drinks orange juice, but sometimes she drinks grapefruit juice. My cousin Martin loves hot chocolate. And he drinks lemonade on hot days. My cousin Dulce drinks a lot of water, but she doesn't drink tap water. She only drinks water from the supermarket. As for me, I drink a lot of tea, both hot and iced. I also drink water, of course, both from the supermarket and from the tap. To tell you the truth, I don't taste any difference between them.

Page 55 (Lesson 3, Activity 7)

Listen *Listen to the conversations from the Downtown International Restaurant. Pretend you are the waiter or waitress. Write down the orders you hear on the check below. Include the price. Add up the check.*

Woman 1: Would you like something to drink to start?

Man: Just water is fine for me, thank you.

Woman 2: I would like a glass of diet soda.

Woman 1: Are you ready to order?

Man: Yes. We'd like some soup to start.

Woman 1: What kind would you like?

Woman 2: I'd like the lobster bisque.

Man: And I'll have the minestrone.

Woman 2: And then I'll have your shrimp tempura.

Man: And I'd like to try the lasagna.

Woman 1: Great.. I'll bring the soups right away.

(pause)

Woman 1: Would you like to see the dessert menu?

Man: No, that's all right. We know what we want.

Woman 2: I'd like to try your cheesecake.

Woman 1: Good choice. It's delicious.

Man: And I'd like the tiramisu.

Woman 1: Another good choice. I'll be right back with them.
Would either of you like coffee?

Man: Yes. Two espressos, please.

Page 57 (Chapter 3 Review, Activity 1)

Read and Listen *Read the story. Then listen to the story.*

Delicious!

Jessica misses some of the food she used to eat in Colombia. She misses her mother's coconut rice the most. But she likes the supermarkets and restaurants in her new neighborhood very much. When she has time, she likes to walk slowly around a supermarket and look at all the different kinds of delicious food they have. And she loves to taste new things. Last night she tried an avocado, a Thai chicken salad, and some grilled swordfish for the first time, and they were all delicious.

Jessica really likes eating at new restaurants. But tonight she isn't going to a restaurant. She is going to stay home and cook. She is going to surprise her family by making her special Colombian soup. She is going to include some pieces of chicken and a few carrots. She is going to add a couple of potatoes, a tomato, and some mushrooms. And then she's going to put in a little salt and some special Colombian spices. It is going to be delicious!

Page 60 (Chapter 3 Review)

Pronunciation *Reduction: Gonna instead of going to*

Many native speakers join words together when they speak. They make two words sound like one word. Native speakers often say *gonna* instead of *going to*.

A. *Listen and repeat the following sentences.*

The family's going to have dinner.

Jessica's going to set the table.

She's going to make potatoes.

They're going to have ice cream.

B. *Work with a partner. Tell your partner some things you are going to do. Say gonna instead of going to.*

Chapter 4: **Housing**

Page 63 (Chapter Opening)

Listen *Listen and repeat each word. Then point to each item in the picture.*

yard
fireplace
garden
grill
mantle
garage
wall unit
bedspread
sofa
dresser
night table
alarm clock
floor lamp
skylight
photos
desk
end table
coffee table
pillows
mini blinds

Page 67 (Lesson 1, Activity 8)

Listen *Listen to the following words. How many syllables do you hear? Write the words in the correct column below.*

Woman 1: New, safe, busy, comfortable, dark, sunny, interesting, beautiful, old, expensive, pretty, ugly

Listen *Mara lives in Manhattan and is thinking about moving to Brooklyn. She is thinking about her apartment in Manhattan and an apartment in Brooklyn. She needs to decide which one is better. Listen to the conversation. Fill in the missing information about the two apartments below.*

Mara: Well, the first thing is that the building in Manhattan is pretty old. At least fifty years old, I think. The building in Brooklyn is only ten years old, and it looks modern. It's also up on the 8th floor and has a view. I like that. And the apartment is air conditioned!

Woman 2: What floor is the Manhattan apartment on?

Mara: It's on the first floor—on street level.

Woman 2: Is there a laundry room in the new apartment building?

Jennifer: Yes, but there isn't a laundry room in my building in Manhattan. There is a laundromat across the street.

Woman 2: Is Brooklyn a safe neighborhood?

Jennifer: Yeah, it's very safe. Manhattan might be a little dangerous, with the apartment right on the first floor. But the Manhattan apartment is not far from my job and some nice restaurants. The Brooklyn apartment is only $850 a month for a pretty nice apartment. I pay $1,200 for my apartment in Manhattan. Brooklyn is closer to a nice beach, but it's a little far from work. With the crowded subways and buses it will probably take an hour to get to work every morning. Which one do you think sounds better?

Woman 2: I don't know, Mara. It's your decision.

Listen *Listen to the conversations. Fill in the missing information in the rental ads below.*

Number 1

Woman 1: Hello, I'm calling about your ad for a studio apartment downtown. Is it still available?

Man 1: Yes, it is.

Woman 1: Can you tell me more about it?

Man 1: Sure. It has a new stove and refrigerator. It's a nice modern kitchen. It also has a large yard with a beautiful garden.

Woman 1: That's nice. How much is the rent, please?

Man 1: It's $850 a month.

Woman 1: Thank you.

Number 2

Man 1: Good morning. Can I help you?

Man 2: Yes. I'm calling about the two-bedroom, two-bath apartment I saw in the newspaper.

Man 1: Yes, it's still available. It's a third-floor apartment in a new building. It has a very nice view.

Man 2: How about the kitchen. Is it a small kitchen?

Man 1: No, it has a large kitchen and a large bathroom, too. It also has a pool.

Man 2: And the rent?

Man 1: It's one thousand a month, plus utilities.

Number 3

Woman 2: I'm calling about the three-bedroom townhouse I saw advertised.

Man 1: Yes, it's very nice. It has two large baths. And it's in a great neighborhood. The neighborhood alone is worth the price.

Woman 2: Can you tell me a little more about the apartment?

Man 1: Sure. It has a balcony and a fireplace. And outside there is an exercise room, a pool, and a large Jacuzzi. This one is a must-see apartment.

Woman 2: How much is the rent?

Man 1: It's thirteen hundred a month.

Page 77 (Chapter 4 Review, Activity 1)

Read and Listen *Read the dialogue. Then listen to the dialogue.*

Moving to a New Apartment

Tania: Hi, Jessica. I came over to tell you that I'm moving to a new apartment.

Jessica: "You're moving? Why?"

Tania: Many reasons. First of all, my apartment needs a lot of repairs, and my landlord isn't very good about making them. Also, the bedroom is too dark. The kitchen is very, very old. And the bathroom isn't big enough. My new apartment is better; it has a nicer and prettier living room and a great view of the neighborhood. It has three big windows, and my old apartment only has one!

Jessica: What about the neighborhood? Is it as nice as this one?

Tania: Well, this neighborhood *is* more interesting, I think. The people are younger and friendlier, but the neighborhood is farther away from the beach. The new neighborhood is cleaner and safer, and is closer to the beach. You know how much I love the beach.

Jessica: What about the rent? Is it more expensive?

Tania: Well, yes. It's $200 more a month. The utility bills will be higher, too. But it's going to be closer to my work, so I won't be late as much.

Jessica: That sounds great. When can I visit you?

Page 80 (Chapter 4 Review)

Pronunciation *Short /i/ sound and long /e/ sound*

Listen to the vowel sounds in these words. Some words have the short /i/ as in the word *live*. Others have the long /e/ sound as in the word *leave*.

A. *Listen and repeat.*

his	sit	cheap
feet	chip	seat
eat	he's	it
lick	fit	leak

B. *Now listen to these word pairs. If the words are the same, write S. If they are different, write D.*

1. he's, he's
2. lick, leak
3. feet, fit
4. chip, chip
5. eat, it
6. he's, his
7. seat, sit
8. lick, lick
9. eat, eat
10. chip, cheap

Chapter 5: **The Past**

Page 83 (Chapter Opening, Activity 1)

Read and Listen *Look at the pictures and read the story. Then listen to the story.*

Yesterday

Yesterday was a typical weekday for Jessica. She usually gets up early during the week and yesterday she got up at 6:30. She always takes a shower before work, and she took one yesterday. She almost always drives to work and she drove yesterday, too. Most days she drinks a cup of coffee in the morning and she drank one yesterday. Most weekdays she works from 8:30 a.m. to 5:30 p.m. and she worked the same hours yesterday. On Monday nights she likes to cook dinner with her aunt and she cooked dinner with Lupe yesterday, too. At night she watches the news on TV at 10:00, and she watched it last night. But, there was something different about her day yesterday. On most weekdays Jessica eats lunch with her coworkers. But yesterday she ate lunch with the handsome director of an animation company. Maybe yesterday wasn't a typical weekday for Jessica after all!

Page 85 (Lesson 1, Activity 3)

Listen *Listen and repeat the verbs. Practice the different ending sounds.*

Woman 1: walked, worked, cooked, baked

Man 1: played, cleaned, cried, called

Woman 1: wanted, needed, rested, painted

Page 85 (Lesson 1, Activity 4)

Listen *Listen to the pronunciation of the following verbs. Write each verb in the correct column.*

Woman 1: washed, smiled, planted, brushed, listened, fixed, tried, talked, decided

Page 86 (Lesson 1, Activity 8)

Listen *Listen to the sentences and write the verb you hear. Then circle if the time is yesterday or every day.*

Man 1: I watched TV.

Woman 1: I work with my brother.

Man 1: I brush my teeth.

Woman 1: I visited my uncle.

Man 1: I wash the dishes.

Woman 1: I played basketball.

Man 1: I rent a two-bedroom apartment.

Woman 1: I wanted to go to a party.

Page 88 (Lesson 2, Activity 2)

Listen *Listen and repeat the present and past of these irregular verbs.*

PRESENT	PAST
be	was/were
begin	began
break	broke
bring	brought
buy	bought
catch	caught
choose	chose
cut	cut
do	did
draw	drew
drink	drank
drive	drove
fall	fell
find	found
fly	flew
get	got
give	gave
go	went
grow	grew
have	had
hear	heard
know	knew
leave	left
make	made
meet	met
pay	paid
read	read
ride	rode
run	ran
say	said
see	saw
sell	sold
send	sent
sing	sang
sleep	slept
speak	spoke
swim	swam
take	took
tell	told
wear	wore
win	won
write	wrote

Page 93 (Lesson 3, Activity 4)

Listen *Listen and fill in the blanks in Habib's story.*

Man 1: Habib got his first job in the United States five years ago. He sold T-shirts and sunglasses from a little stand at the beach. Then three years ago he met a man named Sam. Sam gave him a better job as a clerk in his grocery store. Then two years ago Habib found a job as an assistant manager in a larger grocery store. One year later he became the night manager. Then six months ago he got a big raise and became the store manager.

Page 97 (Chapter 5 Review, Activity 1)

Read and Listen *Read the story. Then listen to the story. Circle the past tense verbs.*

Jessica's Interesting Day

Jessica had a very interesting day last Saturday. In the afternoon she rode her bicycle to the beach. It was a warm, sunny day, so when she got to the beach she stopped at an outdoor café. She took out her pen and started to draw. She drew a picture of the beach with the palm trees in the front and the ocean in the background. She added a young couple talking near one of the palm trees. When she finished, she heard a man's voice over her shoulder. "That's beautiful," he said. "You are very talented." She smiled.

They talked about art for a while. His name was Jack. He knew a lot about art. And he was very nice, too. She enjoyed talking to him. Later, when Jessica left the café, she passed an art gallery around the corner. The paintings in the window were very good so she decided to go in. She walked slowly around the gallery and looked at each picture for a long time. Then she heard Jack's voice again. "I hope you like them," he said. "They're mine." He told her he was an artist, but he also worked as the art director of a computer animation company. "Really?" Jessica said. "I work for a computer animation company too."

Later, he offered to drive her home.

"No, thanks," she said. "I have my bicycle here."

"I enjoyed talking to you," he said. "Would you like to give me your phone number so we can talk again some time?"

She thought about it for a few seconds. "No," she said, "I don't think so."

"OK," he said, "but, please, take my card."

He gave her his business card. She got on her bicycle. She put the card into her shirt pocket.

Page 100 (Chapter 5 Review)

Pronunciation *Past tense endings with the sounds t, d, and id. You will hear a list of nine verbs. Listen carefully to the past tense verb endings. Write each past tense verb in the correct column.*

1. watched, watched
2. smiled, smiled
3. wanted, wanted
4. cleaned, cleaned
5. rested, rested
6. wished, wished
7. pushed, pushed
8. painted, painted
9. tried, tried

Page 103 (Chapter Opening)

Read and Listen *Look at the pictures and read the story. Then listen to the story below. Complete the chart.*

Holidays

Jessica enjoyed the holidays during her first year in the United States. She went skiing at Big Bear Mountain on New Year's Day. She went hiking and camping on Memorial Day. She went swimming at Malibu Beach on Independence Day. And of course, she went dancing on Valentine's Day. During spring break, she went sightseeing in San Francisco. That was a lot of fun.

She also went to some nice holiday parties and events. On Halloween she went to a costume party, and on Thanksgiving she went to a family party at her aunt's house. She also helped decorate her aunt's house for the holidays in December. And on New Year's Eve she had a great time at the street festival. She saw a concert and a fireworks show. She is looking forward to some more enjoyable holidays next year.

Page 108 (Lesson 2, Activity 1)

Listen *Listen to the national weather report. Write the missing temperatures on the map.*

Man: Let's take a quick look at the overall weather picture in the U.S. today. Starting in the South where things were sizzling. In sunny Miami the high for the day was 95, with a night time low of 80. In Atlanta it was cloudy and a little cooler, with a high of 72 and a low of 60. Up in the nation's capitol it was rainy with a high of 55. New York, the Big Apple, also had rain and a daytime high of 45 degrees. The picture in the Midwest was a lot cooler. Chicago had a daytime high of only 30 degrees and a night time low of 25, with some light snow. In Dallas and other parts of Texas, it was a little warmer, with a high of 55 and a low of 42. Over on the West Coast, beautiful weather in Los Angeles with a high of 92. But in San Francisco with the usual cloud cover the high only reached 62 degrees, to go with a night time low of 50.

Page 110 (Lesson 2, Activity 5)

Listen *Listen to the conversation. Write the weather and temperature you hear for each city.*

Man: We have a four-day weekend. Let's take a nice vacation somewhere. What do you think?

Woman: That sounds wonderful. How about four days in London?

Man: I don't know. It's raining in London right now. It may rain the whole four days. And it's cold. 45 degrees yesterday.

Woman: Too cold. How about Paris?

Man: Paris is a little warmer. But it's cloudy there too and the forecast is for rain tomorrow or the next day. And it's only 48 degrees.

Woman: How about Mexico City? I love Mexico City. It is so interesting, and I love Mexican food.

Man: We've been to Mexico City already. I know it's sunny and 60 degrees, and that's great weather. But I'd rather go some place different. Some place new.

Woman: How about Tokyo? No, I guess that's too far for a short vacation. But it *is* warm—almost 70, but partly cloudy. How about Barcelona?

Man: Barcelona? Spain.

Woman: It's usually warm in Spain this time of year. What does it say about Spain?

Man: Yesterday was warm. 80 degrees. But tomorrow . . . cloudy with a chance of rain.

Woman: You know what? Rain isn't so bad. It can be very romantic, if you're with the right person. Don't you think?

Man: OK. Let's go to Barcelona. Call the travel agent!

Listen *Listen and write the missing numbers in the train schedule.*

Woman: I'm interested in going to Washington. Can you tell me what time the Silverstreak arrives in Washington?

Man: The Silverstreak 1 arrives at 6:30 P.M. But there is also a Silverstreak 2 that leaves Boston at 1:30 P.M. That one transfers in New York and arrives in Washington at 10:48 P.M.

Woman: How much is a ticket?

Man: Round trip, Boston to Washington, is $138.

Man 2: Does the Scenic Cruiser 1 go directly from Boston to Washington?

Man 1: No. You have to transfer in New York. It arrives in New York at 2:05 and you take the 2:30 from New York to Washington.

Man 2: How about the later train? When does that arrive in New York?

Man 1: 4:45. And leaves at 6:00 P.M.

Man 2: How much is the round-trip fare?

Man 1: $75 round trip.

Listen and Write *Listen to the story. Write the verbs you hear in the blanks.*

Vacations

Several of Jessica's classmates took interesting vacations last year. Her friend, Lin took a vacation in the fall. She went to the Grand Canyon in Arizona for three days. The weather was great. The temperature was 75 degrees during the day and 55 degrees at night. The views in the Grand Canyon were fantastic. She went hiking and camping but she didn't go fishing. She doesn't like fishing very much. She does like horseback riding very much. One afternoon she rode a horse next to the Colorado River for several hours. That was her favorite part of the trip.

Jessica's friend Alex took his vacation in the winter. He went to Florida for a week. He stopped in Orlando for the first two days. Then he drove down to Miami. He saw a lot of beautiful places along the way. He swam in the ocean in Daytona Beach and again in Ft. Lauderdale. In Miami he went to nightclubs and danced and danced. He met a lot of friendly and interesting people there.

Elham and her husband, Hamed, wanted to save some money, so they stayed at home for their vacation. They slept late, went to the library, saw a few movies, and ate at a new restaurant. The weather was nice so they did some gardening and went for walks in different neighborhoods. They also rearranged their apartment. They had a great time and felt relaxed. And they didn't have to unpack a suitcase at the end of their vacation!

Pronunciation *Reduction: Didjuh instead of did you*

Many native speakers join words together when they speak. They make two words sound like one word. Native speakers often say didjuh instead of did you.

A. *Listen and repeat the following sentences.*

Where did you go?
Did you go to New York?
What did you do there?
Did you have a good time?

B. *Work with a partner. Ask your partner some questions with Did You. Say didjuh instead of did you.*

Page 123 (Chapter Opening, Activity 1)

Read and Listen *Look at the picture of the department store. Read Jessica's story. Then listen to her story.*

Shopping Plans

It is a week before the winter holidays. Jessica and Dulce are going to the big sale at the Downtown Department Store. Dulce wants to go to the men's department. She will probably buy a shirt for her dad. Then she'll go to the jewelry department to get something for her mom. She might buy a pair of earrings or she might buy a nice necklace. Or she might buy her some perfume in the cosmetics department. Then she'll go alone to the entertainment section where she'll buy a CD for Jessica.

Jessica will go to the electronics department where she might buy a portable CD player for her uncle, if it isn't too expensive. She probably won't go to the toy section, but she will definitely go to the housewares section to get a toaster for her aunt. And she'll go to sporting goods where she might get a fishing rod for her cousin, Martin. She won't look at the stoves in the appliance section. She will go to Customer Service to return a shirt that's too big. Then she'll go to the women's department and look for a cute sweater for Dulce. She might look for a cute shirt for herself, but she probably won't buy it. She probably won't have any money left!

Page 130 (Lesson 2, Activity 4)

Listen *Listen and check your answers to Activity 3. Then practice the questions and answers with a partner.*

Man: 1. When will Arnold be back?
Woman: He'll probably be back soon.
Man: 2. When will Jennifer get a job?
Woman: She'll probably get a job next summer.
Man: 3. When will you go to the supermarket?
Woman: I'll probably go to the supermarket tomorrow.
Man: 4. What will Jack buy Jill for her birthday?
Woman: He'll probably buy her a card.
Man: 5. What will Lucy get from the men's department?
Woman: She'll probably get a shirt for her husband.
Man: 6. What will Rosa buy from sporting goods?
Woman: She probably won't buy a skateboard.
Man: 7. When will Cindy and Alberto get married?
Woman: They probably won't get married this year.
Man: 8. When will Davinder visit her mother-in-law?
Woman: She probably won't visit her very soon.

Page 135 (Lesson 3, Activity 7)

Listen *Listen to the radio commercials. Write in the missing information on the ads below.*

Man: Don't miss out on Z Mart's big 4th of July weekend sale. For three days only you will find sales like this: All Cordless telephones 20 percent off, this weekend only. These are regularly priced at $50, but the Z Mart sale price this weekend is $40, but we're not finished there. This weekend only Z Mart will offer an additional 25 percent discount. That's an additional 10 dollars off our already low price. Buy today for only $30!! ...this weekend only at our big 4th of July weekend sale.

Woman: This week only...don't miss our supersale. All sports shoes are reduced, this week only, by 20 to 40 percent. All Pike Superstar running shoes will be 20 percent off this week. Originally priced at 100 dollars, reduced to 80 dollars and this week only take 20 percent more off of that price. This week only you pay 64 dollars, an additional 16 dollar savings. Don't miss it!

Page 137 (Chapter 7 Review, Activity 1)

Read and Listen *Read the story. Then listen to the story.*

Shopping Day

Jessica and her family went shopping today at Downtown Department Store. Jessica bought the prettiest blouse she could find for her cousin Dulce. Her birthday is next week. Martin bought the coolest surfboard. It wasn't the most expensive surfboard, but it wasn't the cheapest either. Uncle Roberto bought three of the most interesting CDs he could find. Jessica's aunt tried on some perfume. Then she went to the jewelry department and saw some pretty silver earrings with purple stones. She liked them better, so she bought them instead.

Jessica bought a box of the most delicious Belgian chocolates for her teacher. She also bought some very nice things for a couple of her classmates and for a couple of her coworkers who are having a New Year's Eve party. She knows that this New Year's Eve won't be the best one of her life because she is homesick. She misses her friends and family in Colombia a lot. But she has a lot of people in Los Angeles she cares about, too, so it won't be the worst New Year's Eve of her life either.

Page 137 (Chapter 7 Review, Activity 3)

Listen *Listen and repeat the three forms of the adjectives from the story.*

pretty	prettier	prettiest
cool	cooler	coolest
expensive	more expensive	most expensive
cheap	cheaper	cheapest
interesting	more interesting	most interesting
delicious	more delicious	most delicious
good	better	best
bad	worse	worst

Page 139 (Chapter 7 Review)

Pronunciation *The /b/ sound vs. the /v/ sound*

The b sound is made with the two lips. The v sound is made with teeth and the bottom lip.

A. *Practice making these two sounds.*

B. *Listen and repeat. Notice the difference between the b sound and the v sound.*

boat vote	berry very
bow vow	base vase
best vest	ban van
bet vet	curb curve

C. Now listen to pairs of words. If they are the same, write S. If they are different, write D.

1. very berry	6. best best
2. base vase	7. vet bet
3. van van	8. base base
4. curve curve	9. bow vow
5. vote boat	10. vote vote

Chapter 8:
Health and Safety

Page 143 (Chapter Opening, Activity 1)

Read and Listen *Read the story. Look at the picture. Then listen to the story.*

Emergency!

Alex had a terrible day yesterday. He was in a car accident on his way to work. He had to call 911 to report the emergency. A woman didn't see a "One Way" street sign and crashed into his car. Unfortunately, Alex wasn't wearing his seat belt so he hit his head on the windshield and cut his forehead. After a few minutes, two Emergency Medical Technicians arrived. They put the woman on a stretcher and took her blood pressure, pulse, and temperature. Then they put her in the ambulance and took her to the hospital. They took Alex to the hospital, too. "You might have a concussion," they said. The woman didn't obey a safety sign and Alex didn't obey a safety rule so now they were both going to the hospital.

Page 146 (Lesson 1, Activity 5)

Listen *Listen and check your answers to activity 4 on page 145. Then listen again and repeat for pronunciation.*

1. neck, 2. shoulders, 3. chest, 4. stomach, 5. leg, 6. knee, 7. foot, 8. arm, 9. wrist, 10. hand, 11. fingers, 12. toes. 13. back, 14. elbow, 15. waist, 16. hips, 17. thigh, 18. calf, 19. ankle, 20. heel, 21. forehead, 22. eyebrow, 23. eyelid, 24. eye, 25. ear, 26. earlobe, 27. lips, 28. nose, 29. mouth, 30. teeth, 31. chin

Listen *Listen to the interview with Alex about his car accident. Fill in the missing information on the form.*

Woman: What was the date of the accident?

Alex: September 20, 2005.

Woman: And the time?

Man: It was 5:45 PM.

Woman: And the location of the accident? It was the intersection of Beach Street and Ocean Avenue. Is that right?

Man: Yes. In Santa Monica, California.

Woman: Right. Were you injured in the accident?

Man: Yes, I was.

Woman: Where were you injured…what part of your body? And what kind of injuries were they?

Man: Well, I cut my forehead. And I also hurt my shoulder. I have some painful bruises on my shoulder.

Woman: Did the accident occur while you were at work or while performing job duties?

Man: Yes, I was performing my job duties.

Woman: Were there other people involved in the accident?

Man: Yes. The driver of the other car.

Woman: Okay. Describe in your own words now what happened in the accident.

Man: It was a car accident. I was driving north on Beach Street when a woman turned the wrong way on a one-way street and hit me. My head hit the windshield and I cut my forehead. I also bruised my shoulder.

Read and listen. *Read the story. Then listen to the story.*

The Earthquake

When Jessica thinks about emergencies, she usually thinks about the earthquake she experienced when she was in high school. She was sitting in her classroom when she heard a loud crack and the whole classroom started to shake violently. Her friend Maura was writing on the blackboard when the earthquake hit. She dropped the chalk and screamed. While the room was shaking, Jessica put her head under her desk. One of her classmates—Oscar—got up and tried to run out of the room. He fell and broke his arm.

The earthquake experience taught Jessica a few things. She learned that you shouldn't try to run during an earthquake. You must get down under something strong and cover your head. And you must not panic! Panic puts everybody in more danger. She also learned that you should have a flashlight and bottled water at home. And she learned that you must have a first-aid kit just in case somebody does get hurt.

Listen *Listen and write the correct number under each picture.*

Man: 1. Rosa was driving to work at 8:15 yesterday morning.

2. It was raining. The speed limit was 35 and she was driving too fast.

3. She was talking on her cell phone. She didn't see a dog running into the street in front of her.

4. She turned to avoid the dog, but she crashed into a tree.

5. She wasn't wearing her seat belt so her head hit the windshield and her chest and shoulder hit the steering wheel.

6. A young woman came to help. She called 911 on Rosa's cell phone.

7. An ambulance arrived a short time later.

8. The paramedics put her on a stretcher and checked her vital signs.

9. Then they took her to the hospital.

Pronunciation *Silent letters*

Many words in English have silent letters. These are letters you see on paper but don't pronounce.

Listen and repeat the words below.

knee	wrist	calf	elbow
neck	waist	back	thigh

Now cross out the silent letters in each word. Check your answers with a partner.

Chapter 9: **On the Job**

Read and Listen *Read the story. Look at the pictures. Listen to the story.*

Many people work at the Downtown Supermarket. Cindy works in the bakery department. She makes and serves coffee and pastries to customers, too. Ralph is the store butcher. He cuts and wraps the meat and sometimes helps customers decide what kind of meat to buy. He knows a lot about different kinds of meat. Tomás works in the office. He is the store manager. He hires and **fires** workers and completes the employee evaluations. Tomás fills out an employee evaluation form for each employee once a year. Rosa works in the office. Her title is Office Assistant. She makes the weekly work schedule and reports the hours for all the employees. Lupe is a cashier. She takes money from the customers and gives them **change**. Timmy helps her at the checkout stand. He bags the groceries when the store is busy. He **stocks** the shelves, too.

Listen *Listen to the sentences and circle the words you hear.*

Man: One. Give it to Maria. It's hers.
Woman: Two. Let's not go out to dinner . Why don't you come to our place?
Man: Three. The little red Doyota is theirs.
Woman: Four. Please give it to me. It's mine.
Man: Five. I asked very nicely and she lent me her book.

Listen *Listen to Tomás talking to four of his employees. Complete the evaluation form below. Use these words: Excellent, Good, Fair, and Poor.*

Tomás: Well, Betsy, for the most part your evaluation is very good. Your attendance, and appearance, are excellent. And of course you get along great with everyone here, so that's excellent too. Your work habits are good. But your punctuality is poor. That's something you're going to have to work on.

Tomás: This is your employee evaluation form, Carla. Of course you get along great with everyone so that category is excellent. Your attendance, appearance, and work habits are good. No problems there. But your punctuality is only fair. You're going to have to improve on that.

Tomás: Well, Timmy, this is your evaluation. Most of the categories are good. Only two late arrivals so your punctuality is good. Your appearance is good. And you get along well with everyone. The problems are your attendance and your work habits.

Tomás: Luis, your evaluation is great as usual. Attendance is excellent – you haven't been out all year. Punctuality too is excellent and your work habits are excellent. You are a very hard worker. Your appearance is professional and you get along well with co-workers so that's rated "good" too. No problems. It's an excellent evaluation. Keep up the good work.

Listen *Listen to the conversations. Complete the messages below.*

Woman 1: Yes, I need to leave a message for Ms. Carter. This is Tania Petrova. That's P-e-t-r-o-v-a. My message is that I'm going to be late for the sales meeting today. I have car trouble. But I should be there by about 10:15. OK. Thank you very much.

Woman 2: This is a message for Bill, from Mary. Please inform Bill that I am sorry but I can't have dinner with him tonight. I have a budget meeting at 7:00. Thank you.

Man: I would like to leave a message for Mr. Ryan. This is Alex Marenko. Please tell Mr. Ryan that I am going to be absent on Monday. Again, I am going to be absent on Monday. I have to go to the doctor. Thank you.

Page 177 (Chapter 9 Review, Activity 1)

Read and Listen *Read the story. Then listen to the story.*

"Can We Talk?"

After her first month at her new job, Jessica received her first employee evaluation. Her supervisor, Ms. Clark, came to Jessica's desk. "I have your one-month employee evaluation," she said. "Can we talk after lunch?"

"Yes, of course," Jessica said.

Jessica worried for the next two hours. She didn't eat lunch. When she went to Ms. Clark's office at 1:00, her hands were shaking. She sat down on the other side of her supervisor's desk. Ms. Clark picked up an evaluation form. Jessica's face felt hot. "Is that one mine?" she asked.

Ms. Clark smiled. "Yes, it's yours. But don't worry. You're doing great."

"I am?"

Ms. Clark looked at the form. "Well, your attendance is perfect. You get along great with everyone. And you're a hard worker."

Jessica's hands stopped shaking. "Thank you," she said.

"There is one small problem," Ms. Clark said. "You came in late twice this month."

"I'm sorry about that," Jessica said. "The traffic was really bad a couple of mornings. I'll try to leave earlier."

"OK," Ms. Clark said. "Here's your evaluation. Keep up the good work."

"Thank you," Jessica said. "I will."

Page 179 (Chapter 9 Review)

Pronunciation *Reductions: him and her become 'im and 'er*

Many native speakers drop beginning sounds when they use the object pronouns him and her. For example, Pick him up becomes Pick 'im up.

A. *Listen and repeat the following sentences.*

Please drop him off at work.
Wake her up at 8:00.
Bring her back after class.
Pick him up at school.

B. *Work with a partner. Take turns reading the sentences to each other. Say 'im and 'er instead of him and her.*

Chapter 10: **A Better Job**

Page 183 (Chapter Opening, Activity 1)

Read and Listen *Read the story. Look at the pictures. Listen to the story.*

The Job Interview

Alex is applying for a job as a warehouse manager for a big electronics company. He filled out an application and brought his résumé to the interview. He gave the interviewer a firm handshake when she introduced herself to him. Then, as she interviewed him, he kept eye contact with her.

The interviewer asked him about his experience and his skills. After he talked about his skills, she said, "Tell me about your personal interests. How would you describe yourself?" He told her some things about himself. Then she asked why she should hire him. He gave her some good reasons. At the end of the interview, he said, "I'd like to be your next warehouse manager." He hoped he sounded like a supervisor!

Page 187 (Lesson 1, Activity 7)

Listen *Listen for skills or abilities that are required for the jobs below. Then complete the "Help Wanted" ads.*

One

Man: I'm calling about the ad for a full-time salesperson. Can you tell me the requirements for the job?

Woman 1: Yes. You need to have 6 months' experience. We're looking for friendly, energetic people, but that isn't a requirement for the job. Good English skills are required. And you must be able to use a cash register. The hours are Monday to Friday, from 2:00–10:00 P.M.

Two

Woman 2: Hello. I'm calling about the opening for a teacher's aide. Can you tell me about the position?

Woman 1: Of course. First of all, for this job you must be able to type 30 words per minute.

Woman 2: I can do that.

Woman 1: Good communication skills are also necessary. We prefer a patient, friendly person, but that isn't a requirement. But computer literacy *is* required.

Woman 2: OK. How can I apply?

Woman 1: You can apply in person, at the West Valley School. Do you know where that is?

Page 190 (Lesson 2, Activity 4)

Listen *Listen and fill in the missing information on Lin's application form.*

Man: Last name is Tran. First name is Lin. What is your address, Lin?

Woman: 229 Park Avenue. That's in Los Angeles. The zip code is 91303.

Man: How long have you lived at this address?

Woman: For two and a half years.

Man: What is your home phone number? With area code first.

Woman: It's 310-555-3789.

Man: What was the last school you attended?

Woman: It was West Valley Adult School. That's in Los Angeles, California.

Man: When did you attend that school?

Woman: I went there from September, 2000 to June, 2001.

Man: Let me ask a couple of questions about your availability. First, do you want to work full-time?

Woman: Yes, I do.

Man: Part-time?

Woman: No, I'm just looking for a full-time job.

Man: Can you work weekends?

Woman: Yes, I can.

Man: How about evenings?

Woman: No, not after 7:00.

Man: OK, Lin. Now let me ask you about your work history. You said you work for Nation's Bank. When did you start that job?

Woman: I started in June, 2003, and I'm still working there.

Man: What is your job title?

Woman: I'm a bank teller. I cash checks, make change, and help customers at the teller window.

Man: And the last job you had before that—in Vietnam—what were the dates of that job?

Woman: I worked at the Auto Import Company from October, 1999 to April, 2000. I was an accountant.

Man: What were your duties on that job?

Woman: I wrote payroll checks for the employees, and I paid the company bills.

Man: Great. Thank you, Lin.

Page 197 (Chapter 10 Review, Activity 1)

Read and Listen *Read the story. Then listen to the story.*

Thinking Ahead

Jessica likes her job, but she knows that people change jobs a lot in the United States. Sometimes it is necessary to change jobs to get a higher salary or an opportunity to advance. Right now Jessica is happy with her salary. She gets along well with her coworkers, and she likes her boss. Her job is in a very nice location. But her job doesn't have very good benefits. They don't provide health insurance or paid vacation. And there isn't much opportunity for advancement, so in the future she might look and apply for another job.

When she goes on another job interview, she will talk about her computer animation skills and her artistic ability. She can also say that she is a good team player, and that she is very organized and dependable. Sometimes she isn't very punctual, but she won't tell them that!

Listen *Listen to the conversations and fill in the missing information on the "Help Wanted" ads.*

One

Man: I'm calling about the job opening for an office assistant.

Woman: Yes. It is a temporary job in a medical office.

Man: What is required for the job?

Woman: First, you must be able to type 25 words per minute.

Man: OK.

Woman: At least one year experience is also required.

Man: Anything else?

Woman: You also must have good telephone skills. And you must be a team player.

Man: OK. Thank you very much.

Two

Woman 1: I'm calling about the opening for a receptionist.

Woman 2: Yes, it's in an import/export office.

Woman 1: What are the requirements for the job?

Woman 2: You must be organized and punctual. Does that sound like you?

Woman 1: Yes, I'm very organized and punctual. What are the duties of the job?

Woman 2: The duties include greeting customers, some filing, and answering phones.

Woman 1: Anything else?

Woman 2: Nothing else required, but we prefer someone who is a fast learner with good people skills.

Woman 1: Okay. How can I apply?

Pronunciation *Stressing content words*

In English, the most important words in a sentence get more stress than the other words. We call these important words content words. They are said louder and often at a higher pitch than the other words.

A. *Listen and repeat the following sentences:*

Do you want an application?
Eye contact is important.
I drove a truck.
I want to be a receptionist.
Can you work on weekends?

B. *Listen again. This time underline the content words in these sentences.*

C. *Now work with a partner. Practice one of the conversations in this chapter. As you speak, be sure to stress the content words.*

INDEX

ACADEMIC SKILLS